W9-BIT-535

THE HANDBOOK OF HIGH PERFORMANCE DRIVING

THE HANDBOOK OF HIGH PERFORMANCE DRIVING

PRODUCED BY Lyle Kenyon Engel

TEXT BY Deke Houlgate

Introduction by Bob Bondurant

ILLUSTRATED WITH PHOTOGRAPHS

DODD, MEAD & COMPANY NEW YORK

For the automotive enthusiast

Printed in the United States of America
by The Cornwall Press, Inc., Cornwall, N.Y.

Library of Congress Cataloging in Publication Data

Houlgate, Deke, 1905–
The handbook of high performance driving.

1. Automobile driving. I. Engel, Lyle Kenyon.
II. Title.
TL152.5.H67 629.28'3'2 75–22177
ISBN 0–396–07140–6

Contents

Introduction

by Bob Bondurant

I started the Bob Bondurant School of High Performance Driving on February 14, 1968, for several reasons. One, I enjoy driving, both as a sport and as a release for excess energy. Two, high performance driving is a self-expression and an art few people achieve, because they give up trying to reach that level of accomplishment too soon.

After twelve years of both European and American road racing of all types, including the highest level—Formula 1 Grand Prix racing—El Grande Accidente happened back here in the United States at Watkins Glen, New York. It was during a U. S. Road Racing Circuit race for Group 7 Can-Am cars.

A defective steering arm broke—I only discovered this after extensive research—as I was coming out of a 150-mph turn. This caused me to go up and over a dirt bank, shearing the floor out and flipping the car end over end a number of times. I broke both my ankles, shattered my right heel, and suffered several other broken bones. The multiple injuries, of course, put me in the hospital, forcing me to rest and to think.

Gradually, I put my thoughts together. Somewhere in the back of my mind, I guess I had always wanted to teach road racing. If I could put my twelve years of international racing experience to work for others, in an instructional form, I could provide a shortcut to racing knowledge for those people who want to get into racing the correct way.

After thinking further, I began to feel that a lot of the same knowledge could be applied to all people who drive, whether it was racing or on the highway, and so I put together an emergency driving program to deal with all types of everyday driving problems.

I feel that highway safety needs more attention than ever today. Our cars go faster and handle better, but the level of driving skill remains the same. More than 50,000 people are killed every year on our highways, and most people say to themselves, "Too bad," as it hasn't happened to them yet, even though they could be the next victim through someone else's negligence and inexperience.

That's the reason I have developed a most complete advanced highway driving course for both men and women sixteen years and older with a valid driver's license. It's also why I feel that this is a very important and informative book that could help save your life.

Deke Houlgate's reasons for writing this book paralleled my own. To write the book, he attended my school and experienced the same level of training we give aspiring professional racing drivers. At the end of the course we always ask each student what one single important thing he or she believes was learned in a week of instruction, and when we asked Deke, he answered:

"To learn to go fast, first you must learn to go slow."

We never had thought of it that way, but it's true. So is the fact that this country, with all its dependency on the motor vehicle, needs to do something about the quality of its driving. The message in this book is that we can't sit back and pass the buck, let the federal government do it, or the local police, or the insurance companies. We already have proved that nothing gets accomplished that way. If everyone who reads this book would begin *concentrating* and *looking ahead* while sitting at the wheel, we could put an end to a lot of needless killing and pain.

Since this book was written, I have moved my entire driving school to Sears Point International Raceway in Sonoma, California, just forty miles north of beautiful San Francisco. We at the Bondurant School offer complete courses in high performance driving, competition road racing, skid control, and accident preventive (evasive) maneuvers. Anyone who drives, no matter how experienced, will enjoy the experience and will certainly profit from it.

1

The Driving Experience

Wonderful invention, the self-starter. For three-quarters of a century the automobile industry has dedicated itself to making the automobile inexpensive to own, easy to operate, and pleasurable to ride in. The invention that set this process into high gear was Kettering's development of the electric starter. With one swift, almost unconscious motion you can flick a 300-horsepower engine to life. You can. Anyone can.

Sixty years ago starting a motor car was high adventure. In fact, everything about an automobile was exciting. The noise. The fumes. The heady thrill of ripping down the road at an illegal 15 miles an hour. But the most fulfilling accomplishment of all was being able to start the infernal machine. Before the self-starter came into use it was necessary to turn the motor over with a crank. That was sometimes a long, physically exhausting, and painful process. "Cranker's arm," one encased in a plaster cast, was as much a badge of honor as today's "skier's leg."

With mass production, more automobiles became available, they were cheaper to buy and easier to drive, and many were delivered into the hands of poor drivers. With driving less of a drudgery, the demand for cars far exceeded the ability of the nation's road system to carry traffic and the ability of the licensing authorities to deal with individual differences in driving skills. Government has found itself increasingly more helpless to cope with the epidemic of highway death. Accidents with motor vehicles have taken more lives than all the wars fought by America throughout history.

A tremendous amount of development has gone into improving the automobile, refining the fuel it consumes, making the highways and streets on which it runs more efficient, and—in recent years—in reducing the relatively adverse effects the automobile has on the environment. By contrast, the "traffic safety establishment" has devoted most of its energies to worthless advertising campaigns to brainwash drivers. ("Speed kills!", "If you drink, don't drive!", "The life you save may be your own!"), while at the same time squandering nickels and dimes on education in its puny efforts to do something about improving driver performance.

If you are a beginning driver, you must become aware of the fact that, while you probably had the benefit of some training in a public school or under the direction of a licensed private instructor before you could apply for your license, very few drivers on the road today have had even that much instruction. The instruction given to beginning drivers is concentrated in two areas: familiarizing the student with traffic law and custom, and teaching him the basics of operating an automobile. The chances are good that few high-school driver education teachers are even interested enough in their subject to cover correct seating position (if they knew what that was) and holding the steering wheel properly. As for the private commercial instructor, he has a special objective, making the student confident enough at the wheel to pass an examination for a driver's license. The teacher might wish to go beyond that stage and really teach students how to drive a car, but in his business, time is money, and he can't afford to squander special instruction on an individual student unless the student has money to pay for it. The private instructor may be limited by other factors: his disinterest, lack of pride in his work, or lack of ability to go beyond teaching basic driving skills.

So you get your first driver's license, and you move out into traffic on your own for the first time. To many new license holders that is a frightening experience as well as an exhilarating one. In the transition from "student driver" to "licensed driver" one learns quickly the hypocrisy of highway safety. On the one hand, speed limits, traffic law enforcement, and other restrictions on the use of a motor vehicle are supposed to prevent accidents, injuries, and death. On the other hand, people crash and sometimes get hurt or even killed without exceeding posted speed limits or breaking any other laws. You learn quickly that in the real world of everyday driving nearly every car on the road violates most speed limits and nearly every driver breaks traffic laws without apparently endangering anybody.

Part of the reason for this is that traffic laws have developed without serious regard for their effect on overall driver performance, while driver training has little improved from those early days, when to learn how to drive was to go out in the country with Dad and sit behind the wheel on a deserted road, learn how to start the car, stop it, and keep it on the right side of the pavement. Some people who ignore posted speed limits and coast through stop signs are not equipped, for one reason or another, to accept regulation, but most drivers on the road drive at their own speed and cut occasional corners around the law, because consciously or subconsciously they can't understand the safety logic of some traffic laws. They feel safe. Their experience tells them they are safe. Quite often they are safe.

Driver training and driver licensing fit neatly into this pattern of inconsistency. The official attitude toward driver training in most states is that it is an exercise to prevent new drivers from going out and killing people on the highway. Licensing is regarded as a source of revenue. It's no wonder that many motorists regard their driving skills rather matter-of-factly. Any skill a driver may acquire has to be developed in practice after he receives his license, and often the experience he needs to avoid difficulties must be obtained during the emergency he should have been trained to face. As Ken Dunipace of the National Highway Traffic Safety Administration puts it, "Most people have no more thought about the driving task they are performing than if they were going in a room and turning on a television set."

The standard of driver education is called "thirty and six." It means that to complete a course that leads to licensing a high-school-age driver, it is necessary for him or her to attend thirty hours of classes and have six hours of practical behind-the-wheel experience.

That isn't very much, but even those figures are misleading. The thirty hours of classroom instruction are usually given by a teacher who does the job for extra pay or who is so low in seniority he can't get out of the assignment. According to Les Moore, highway safety specialist for the National Highway Traffic Safety Administration:

"In a lot of instances, where a teacher goes in and has to take over the school safety program, maybe it happens to be the youngest teacher. He or she may not have any background or experience at all. They kind of grow into it. They are put in because they are available. Maybe they've had one course in [safety], which doesn't make them an expert."

Adds Ken Dunipace: "An awful lot of driver education people have entirely an education background, and they don't have the technical understanding to recognize vehicle dynamics. You go up and talk to a driver education teacher in high school right now and talk about things as basic as oversteer and understeer, and they don't know what you're talking about."

Thirty hours of lectures by a high-school driver ed teacher aren't, in other words, likely to prepare many Fangios. Now let's examine that six hours behind the wheel.

Chances are that unless the student is exposed to an unusual situation his six hours will include four hours of sitting in the back seat watching another student drive and only two hours of actual driving. Once behind the wheel the student will find himself participating in a familarization, not a training situation. Practically all the driving is done on city streets or public rural roads under ideal traffic conditions. Occasionally an instructor will expose his pupils to the expressway or rush-hour city traffic, but not often or as a deliberate training exercise.

Thirty and six gives the student the rudiments, teaches him what the controls and the instruments mean, more or less indoctrinates him about safety law and custom, and, finally, gives him the feel of controlling a 4000-pound automobile. Chances are that driver ed will provide an automobile that has an automatic transmission, power steering, and power brakes. It is a good bet the instructor doesn't even know how to sit or hold the steering wheel properly, much less have the ability or the inclination to teach those simple exercises.

The cars that are used to teach driver ed are not likely to be typical of the driving experience of the young beginner. A six-cylinder Plymouth or a Chevy Belair will have far different performance characteristics than the VW bug, which the beginning driver may elect as his first purchase. Or a Triumph Spitfire. Or a GTO. Or a Mustang Mach IV. If the beginner drives only the family wheels, his transportation may be a Cadillac or a Dodge pickup with a camper body, and it's unfair to toss him out into traffic under all sorts of weather and lighting conditions with only two to six hours of daylight driving experience and a little practice with his parents in the car.

The sixteen- or seventeen-year-old completing a thirty-and-six course earns a learner's permit that allows him to drive any passenger vehicle so long as there is a licensed adult driver with him. In many cases the teenager with a learner's permit can also legally operate a motorcycle in traffic without an adult accompanying him.

The federal government's highway safety people are trying to correct this situation by changing driver education to include things like accident avoidance and hazardous driving experience; but basically, the bureaucrats in fifty state capitals look at driver ed as an indoctrination process, something to "keep the kids from going out and killing people," while they can't help regarding the licensing process as a commercial enterprise.

In this setup the driving instructor—both the public-school teacher and the private instructor—is a monitor of sorts. His professional standing in the world of education is certainly not as high as the English or algebra teacher in the same high school. There is no encouragement for him to improve his standing, and consequently many driving educators suffer from a lack of appreciation for what they are doing and a resulting lack of pride in their own work. If nobody at the top cares, why should they? To get into "real" driver education, it would be necessary to adopt a lot of the techniques used in the high-performance or race-driving schools. That would be too costly for most school systems, and the term "high performance" is abhorrent to the people who operate them.

To this sort of administrator, the high-performance driving enthusiast is a speed-happy nut. Many police officials would like to clear high-performance cars and drivers off the roads. Traffic research people can produce statistics to show that most high-performance car owners are young, and that most young drivers have a high accident rate. What they fail to take into account is that to the person who likes to drive his motor vehicle, there is a pride that goes with performance. Someone who enjoys driving likes to drive well. And to improve his driving skills he can't turn to the highway safety establishment. He has to either go underground or go racing.

As far as going underground is concerned, one of the most widespread abuses of public roads that exists without apparently endangering society, but in an outlaw capacity nevertheless, is street racing. Every weekend, and on many week nights as well, the street racers gather in drive-ins, supermarket parking lots, and along the boulevards of cities like Los Angeles, Detroit, New York, and Atlanta and plan their racing activities for the early morning hours. One magazine writer even noted that there has been street racing in Wendover, Utah. Many deaths have been caused by foolhardy individuals racing each other on public roads under ordinary traffic conditions, but none have come to our attention that can be attributed to organized street racing.

To state that street racing apparently doesn't kill is not to condone an illegal act, for organized street racing tends to break down respect for traffic laws that govern, even though they don't seem capable of coping with traffic safety. In this country we have a revulsion for using the public roads for speed contests, but when a businessman from Mexico City was shown the Los Angeles freeway system he grew enthusiastic about its potential as a grand super-speedway for high-speed automobiles and wondered why we didn't shut them down to traffic every so often and stage races on them.

The other, more acceptable alternative for the high-performance enthusiast is to get involved with organized racing. Two forms of motor sport are open to any street-licensed driver: drag racing and off-road racing. Road racing, under sanction of the Sports Car Club of America, has recently become available to eighteen-year-olds, and the smaller racing associations also make it possible for eighteen-year-olds to compete. For those younger than eighteen, it is possible to compete in everything from quarter-midgets to go-karts, but there is a great deal more activity for youthful motor racing participants on motorcycles than there is in four-wheel vehicles.

Another low-key and relatively inexpensive performance opportunity open to the licensed driver is the sports car solo event, variously the slalom, gymkhana, autocross, tralom, and hill climb. Each is a slightly different type of timed event on courses where high speeds cannot be achieved. The premium is placed on preparation of a street-legal automobile and on driving skill.

This sort of driving skill is not regularly a part of driver education. The federal government would like to see a slalom-type course added to driver education curricula, because it helps to develop familiarity with a car's performance and makes the driver keenly aware of his capabilities. Unfortunately, the bureaucrats have to keep talking about "driving tasks" and can't relate the managing of an automobile to enjoyment. Many in the NHTSA, the highway safety administration, really do enjoy cars, and the top administrator, Douglas S. Toms, has competed in off-road and drag races, but nobody in the U.S. Department of Transportation is encouraged to promote racing.

To a person who uses his personal transportation as a means to go back and forth to work or as something in which to carry groceries, it's difficult to relate to love of cars and driving. But the true enthusiast understands who and why he is. Are you an enthusiast?

Did you ever wish to return to those thrilling early days of motoring, when yokels yelled, "Get a horse!"? When farmers came storming out of their barns with pitchforks and charged the motor car because their horses and cows were frightened? When the proper gentlemen wore dusters? When the heroes of the day were Victor Hemery and Ralph de Palma and Barney Oldfield and Arthur Duray and Maurice Renault and Camille Jenatzy and Jimmy Murphy?

Have you ever dreamed of flashing across the finish line at Indianapolis Motor Speedway with the roar of 300,000 fans overcoming the high whine of your turbocharged racing motor? Or drinking champagne from a huge silver cup on the victory stand, grimy and exhausted in every muscle after twenty-four hours of driving at Le Mans? Do you get any satisfaction from driving from home to office in the most efficient manner, in the least amount of time, with the senses so concentrated on the pleasurable task of driving that the playing of a car radio is annoying?

Do you take pride in the looks or the working mechanism of your own personal car? Have you ever served on the pit crew for an amateur racer? Have you driven the family wheels out to the drags and raced for bucks, cups, or grudges? Do you pump up the tires and careen through a slalom course on the weekends, or would you like to? Are you addicted to watching the skilled professionals of NASCAR, USAC, or SCCA, and do you try to pick out the good points and the flaws in their driving styles? Do you spend inordinate amounts of money or time taking care of your car, polishing it, buying accessories, modifying its looks and its performance?

Is there something about a classic car, restored to the last button of the seat upholstery, that fascinates you? Do you visit auto museums to gawk at the magnificent dissimilarity of yesterday's product? Do you wish you could own a Cobra or an old Packard or a two-seat T-Bird or a prewar Rolls?

If your answer to any of these questions is yes, then you are that rare individual, the enthuisast, for whom this book was written and to whom it is dedicated. As an enthusiast you are aware of the many problems connected with pursuing your love affair with the automobile. Being an enthusiast costs perhaps more money than you should reasonably lavish on a piece of machinery. The law looks askance at you and perhaps you get the idea that you are occasionally harassed. Your non-enthusiast friends and relations wonder about your good sense. Your supervisor or employer might mark you down as a bit immature and might refer to you as "that hot-rodder" in off-guard moments. You may have to endure the criticism of a spouse or lover, who resents sharing your time and funds with "that car."

But what is so bad about enthusiasm for a fine automobile and its operation? Gary Gabelich, the world's fastest man on wheels, started on his road to immortality by sketching rockets with wheels on them as a grade-school student. Dan Gurney, the son of a Metropolitan Opera baritone, graduated from street racer to international driving star and now has a booming business than was built on his racing career. Don Garlits, who came close to being a high-school dropout, serves as an inspiration to a generation of boys who might have left school themselves except that Big Daddy Garlits urged them not to. George Hurst, whose hand was hopelessly crippled as a sailor, took his mustering-out pay and started an enthusiast-oriented garage that he built into a multimillion-dollar corporation. In other words, there is nothing to be ashamed of if you are an auto enthusiast. You're in good company.

But if you are interested in learning to handle a high-performance automobile, there are very few places for you to go for instruction. Except for the few schools oriented toward race driving, and a handful of others that teach "driving tasks" such as controlled skids and accident avoidance maneuvers, there aren't many convenient places to go. If they were all operating at capacity, together they would be capable of turning out a total of perhaps 200 students a week.

Actually, it is easier to learn how to handle an automobile at or near the limits of its capabilities than it is to master only the skills required of a driver-education graduate. Bob Bondurant proved that. He put his own son through his school for racing drivers, despite the fact that his boy had never driven an automobile in his life. After a few hours of special tutoring and a couple of days of difficult adjustment, young Bobby was just as proficient as the veteran drivers in the same class.

We attended the Bob Bondurant School for High Performance Driving at Ontario Motor Speedway, and we found ourselves overcoming years of bad driving habits developed over more than a half million miles of driving. We don't know which is easier, to start from scratch as Bobby did or to go through a course like this with a lot of experience. Quite quickly we realized that it would be necessary to start with a fresh slate and let the instructor write in everything that should be there. The process started in the "ground school," which preceded our introduction to driving the school cars.

First we learned the basics of the Bondurant technique:

(1) The automobile communicates to the driver through sight, noise, vibration, and the sensation of gravity forces. To get full benefit of what the car is saying, it is important to be able to receive and understand all the information being provided.

(2) Consequently, seating position is very important. The driver receives information from what he sees from his head position, through his hands from the steering wheel, through his feet from the floor and the pedals, and

through his thighs, hips, and back from the seat. A comfortable position, flat against the back of the seat, is important.

(3) Correct hand position on the steering wheel is also essential. The arms should be slightly bent and hands placed at the nine and three o'clock positions, thumbs locked over the top of the steering wheel braces. If the arms are extended straight out the seat is too far back; the driver can't turn the steering wheel easily and thus does not have proper control of the car. If he is sitting too close and the arms are bent 90 degrees or more, the driver likewise does not have control. If he has to turn quickly, his elbows will get in the way.

(4) The automobile is a dynamic thing, always obeying Newton's laws. Once in motion it wants to go straight ahead. The car is affected by every action the driver commits it to. When the brakes are applied, the car wants to continue straight ahead, and weight transfers to the front wheels. This causes the nose to dive and the rear end to lighten. Acceleration causes the reverse, more weight on the rear and a lightening on the front wheels.

When turning to the right, weight transfer is to the left, and vice versa. The driver of a car has the power to control all these actions.

(5) The keynote of efficient vehicle operation (in racing, this means fast lap times) is smoothness. Smooth braking, smooth turning, smooth acceleration, smooth shifting, smooth declutching result in more speed on the race track than any quick movement. In other words, forget about speed shifting, whipsawing the steer-

ing wheel, and pumping or stabbing the brakes, and concentrate on smoothness.

After ground school we had a week of intensive instruction, including more ground school, and practice in a variety of high-performance street and racing cars, about which we will write in later chapters. But the five basic premises of Bondurant's course (most of which are never mentioned in a regular driving school) should be mastered and practiced by all drivers, whether they are planning to work their way up to Formula 1 racing or are interested only in extracting the last iota of pleasure from their personal automobile. Always remember:

The car talks. Listen.
Sit properly.
Hold the wheel properly.
Think about what the car is doing at all times.
Be smooth.

2

Efficiency Is Enjoyment

Near the end of the week at Bob Bondurant's school, our instructor asked each student in the class what he thought was the most important single thing he had learned so far. Almost in reflex, certainly without thinking about it, this writer replied:

"To go fast, first you must learn to go slow."

That is the way the week had gone, certainly from the first "ground school" session through familiarization runs on a tricky oval course, negotiating the accident simulator, and finally on the road course at Ontario Motor Speedway. Even at speeds that suggested you were hanging the car out to within a fraction of an inch of its breakaway point, we were consciously telling ourselves to go slow where it counted. When we didn't, it cost precious fractions and even seconds of lap time, and occasional spins were experienced by all of us.

The temptation in learning to drive a high-performance car is to gloss over the mundane aspects and to concentrate on the enjoyable parts. There is no getting around it. There must be a little speed freak in all of us, because acceleration gives exhilaration, squealing the tires and leaning out in turns quicken the pulse, and sustained high speed gives one a sense of mastery over his environment—which in the case of a high-performance driver is his automobile.

Bondurant's instructor passed a steering wheel around the class and asked each student to hold it, turn it, and get the feel of it. Assuming the proper nine and three o'clock positions for left and right hands, each one of us turned the wheel from left to right and back again. We felt a bit foolish, as if this were a little juvenile. Yet later, in the excitement of a difficult maneuver, every one of us forgot the proper wheel position and grabbed it wrong.

Obviously, there is more to turning the wheel of a car than merely holding on and moving it from side to side. The first thing we had to learn was smoothness, which is achieved by starting every turn slowly and gradually increasing the turning movement. A quick crank of the wheel throws the car out of control quite easily, or at the least, unbalances it enough to make it hard to manage. By practicing smooth motion with the steering wheel, a quick, smooth turn can be learned with little difficulty.

The next time the instructor passed the dummy steering wheel around the classroom, it was to practice hairpin turns. As he demonstrated, the type of simple turn we had practiced was good enough only to crank the wheel halfway around its arc. He was now ready to show us how to turn it all the way around without sacrificing any smoothness. This is how we practiced a left turn, and later how we did it in street and race cars.

We took the left hand off the wheel and moved it over to where the right hand was holding it at the 3 o'clock position, hooking the left thumb under the brace. Sliding the wheel through the motionless right hand, we guided it 180 degrees to the left until the right thumb caught the opposite brace. Now we had hands at nine and three again, although the wheel was turned halfway around. To continue the turn through a complete revolution of the steering wheel, we merely followed through with a normal left turn.

Now the trick was to return the steering wheel to its normal position. First we turned it 180 degrees to the right and found our hands at nine and three, where they belonged. To continue moving the wheel around we brought our right hand over to the nine o'clock position, hooked the thumb under the brace, and slid the steering wheel through the left hand, back to its normal position.

Since going through the Bondurant course, it has been an amusing experience to watch other motorists attack and fight their steering wheels, not aware of their ineptness. It would be a lot funnier, except that twenty-five years of steady driving experience had not taught us any better. We soon realized that we shouldn't be amused at others, only ashamed of ourselves and appalled at the quality of driver education which still fails to equip high-school students with the rudiments of how to hold a steering wheel and how to turn a car efficiently. How tough a job would it be to teach the mechanics of steering? Even pre-school children get the knack of it when they climb inside Daddy's car and stand up in the driver's seat to play a high-speed game of pretend.

At the Bondurant school, the steering wheel was passed around in the classroom because controlling the wheel is only part of the procedure that has to be mastered for going around turns in the most efficient way, and our instructor wanted to make sure we got that right so we could go on to the next step. Turning is more than steering, another misunderstood principle of vehicle operation, one that separates the good high-performance driver from the majority of people on the roads (and a large number of competitors on the road courses, too). Before we ever got into a car to practice control, the instructor brought out a model car and demonstrated some very simple, but almost universally overlooked, principles of vehicle dynamics by pushing the model around on a table with his hand.

Earlier we mentioned weight transfer. It has everything to do with how well a car gets through a corner. Right turns throw weight onto the left side of the car, left turns onto the right; braking throws weight onto the front, and accelerating onto the rear. The faster or tighter the turn, the more the weight transfer.

A car which is turned within its normal capabilities will exhibit neutral steering. It will politely go where it is aimed. Pushing the car toward its limits, however, will bring out one of two dynamic conditions which are, as we might say, not always desirable. One is called understeer, or more simply "plowing," and the other is oversteer, or "hanging the back end out."

Understeer is common to people who drive their cars too fast through corners on the street. The car doesn't turn as much as they want it to, but, unfortunately, the driver usually doesn't know why. The car is telling the driver that it wants to continue in a straight line, and its momentum in that direction won't let it turn as sharply as the driver wants it to. If he'd just slow down a little, the car would respond better.

Oversteer is more common to rear-engine or mid-engine cars. The rear end wants to go in the opposite direction from which the car is being steered, and it is not too serious a condition to any driver who is familiar with handling it. However, it can be disastrous, and was a major plank in the Ralph Nader campaign against the Corvair.

So turning can be hazardous to your health, if you don't know what the car is doing or why. In understeer the car doesn't turn as much as you want it to, and in oversteer it turns too much. How do you handle these two problems? The best way is not to let them happen at all, to drive as close to neutral steer as possible all the time. This means SLOW DOWN.

In a high-performance or competition situation, slowing means braking. Using the brakes does more than reduce the speed of your car. Remember weight transfer? It throws more of the weight onto the front wheels, which are the two doing the steering. For maximum control in a turn, it is necessary to have the weight shifted forward onto the front wheels to give them better traction and to allow surer steering control. At the Bondurant school, this meant that the students in our class had to learn all over again how to use the brakes in their cars.

Without the knowledge and understanding of vehicle dynamics, everybody has his own braking style. Some tend to stay off the brakes and to tap them only occasionally in normal driving. Some stab the brakes hard and then let off. Some drivers drag their feet on the brakes. Some use uneven pressure even when the foot is firmly on the brake pedal, letting up in the middle of braking and coming down hard later. It seems as if most drivers hit their brakes with the same pressure all the time except during panic stops. If they want more braking force, they merely hold the foot down longer. Almost as universally, in panic stop situations, most drivers jam the foot toward the floor until the brakes lock up, then they sometimes don't let up even with all four tires squealing and no steering control.

In braking, the ideal method is to strive for smoothness, getting onto the brakes without stabbing them, but increasing the pressure to the maximum necessary, and either holding or "trailing" the brakes as long as necessary to keep weight on the front wheels in a turn.

That is a mechanical act which is tough to learn properly without the help of an instructor. "Trailing the brakes" means keeping the foot on the brake lightly until the car has gone far enough into the turn so that weight transfer will not be too severe. At that point the car is already set up to get through the turn and needs to be straightened out for rapid acceleration down the straightaway.

Smooth turning requires the precise interaction of foot and hand, braking and steering, both movements done smoothly and in concert with each other. To get the job done right requires a good amount of coordination. Some people, outstanding athletes for example, have more natural coordination than others, but practice can smooth out the jerkiest and sloppiest of techniques.

It's at the point of developing smoothness in a turn that this book leaves off and experience, particularly with a good teacher, must take over. There is nothing more exciting in road racing than to see the perfect execution of a difficult corner, done so smoothly that the faster driver appears as if he is motoring through the turn without a care in the world. No sudden arm movements, no deviations of the car's track from a simple line through the corner. For some drivers, developing this smoothness is as natural as Ella Fitzgerald singing a song, Fran Tarkenton eluding tacklers as he picks out the target for his pass, or Willie Mays swinging at a curve ball. For others, it takes practice, practice, and more practice. But smoothness can be learned! To be a winner on the track or an exceptional driver on the street, it must be learned.

In scientific terms, what the driver does when he turns is to exert a force on an object in motion. In addition to the coordination of foot and hand, he must learn to feel the reaction of the car to this force and to coordinate it perfectly with the car. This is the knack the good race driver has but seldom knows how to describe—"seat of the pants" driving, feeling as if car and driver were one. The attempt to impart this feeling, this understanding between the driver and his machine, range from groping for words to elaborate scientific analysis of turning forces.

Books on race driving sometimes relate cornering forces to such mathematics as Piero Taruffi's

$$F_c = \frac{W}{g} \times \frac{V^2}{r}$$

or Paul Frere's simpler

$$F_c = \frac{m(v^2)}{R}$$

They multiply the mass of the car by the square of its velocity and divide by the radius of the curve to compute the centrifugal force acting on the car. This tells them how fast any corner can be taken by any car. It is great to have this information, as it saves the professional a lot of time learning a new course, but a lot of the arithmetic can be replaced by the report the car gives to the driver through his back, hands, and legs, which is confirmed by the driver's sense of gravity and what he sees through his windshield. Quite often, actual speed through the turn isn't nearly the most essential element of cornering, as we shall see.

Bondurant teaches that you should brake hard for a corner to allow yourself as much time on the straightaway at top speed as possible. Braking lowers the nose and presses the front wheels hard against the pavement for better traction. Trailing the brakes, keeping them lightly on through the turn to keep the nose down, is another essential technique. The final and most important technique that results in good cornering is smooth, rapid acceleration, using as much of the road as possible to increase the length of the straightaway. Thus, the attack of a driver on a road course is one of straightening out turns and increasing the usable amount of straightaway.

Once turning techniques are mastered, the key to high-performance cornering is finding the apex of the turn. The apex, or the point at which the car should be closest to the inside edge of the pavement, should normally be beyond the halfway point of the turn, a position that allows for the best acceleration onto the straightaway. "Finding the apex" becomes one of the most important racing skills.

In road racing, as on public roads, the variety of corners is infinite. Their radii change, their bankings are different, their elevations change. What happens to the road under the wheels of the car also affects vehicle's dynamics and must be worked into that smooth coordination necessary to get high performance out of a car. Some turns produce not one but two apexes, and certain combinations of turns cause the driver to move the apex for one turn from what might be the ideal position to a compromise location in order to get through the series of turns in the shortest possible time.

There is a very practical use for high-performance cornering in the day-to-day traffic situation—driving through freeway on-ramps to reach safe traffic merging speed. Freeway designers typically build hairpin turns into the system and empty them onto through traffic lanes where the speed differentials are sometimes 20 to 25 miles an hour between mortorists already on the freeway and those who are entering the freeway. If you are able to drive onto the freeway without some slowpoke hindering your progress, you are better off getting up to the speed at which traffic is flowing while still on the on-ramp, rather than trying to cut into the traffic lane while still accelerating, thereby causing motorists who are coming up behind you to slow down drastically.

To get the best possible break when entering a freeway, finding the apex for the on-ramp is important. Blending in with moving traffic isn't all that simple. Where is the apex of turn? If you were to drive through any turn and be clocked at the entrance and the exit, the apex would be precisely in the middle to get the best elapsed time. But the object of apexing properly is to cut lap times, so the best apex is a compromise between the fastest speed through a turn and the best acceleration down the next straightaway. To put it another way, one driver may gain half a second in a corner but lose three-quarters of a second down the straight. His net loss could be 2 mph in average speed, and if he does that on every lap it adds up to defeat. If he were to move the apex up to get the best shot at the straightaway, he would lose that half second but maybe win the race.

An important axiom taught at the Bondurant school is that road races are not won in the corners. They are won on the straightaways. If two cars go through a corner in the same elapsed time, but one exits at 40 mph and the other at 45, they will probably have a 5 mph differential all the way down the straight. At the end of the straightaway, when one car is traveling 100, the other is still doing 95. Under those circumstances the fast driver coming out of the turn has disappeared down the track. He's long gone.

Apexing becomes very important, and positioning the car to hit that apex becomes just as critical as low lap times. Putting all the skills together—thinking yourself into the right position to take the turn, locating the proper apex, braking precisely at the right time and slowing enough, proper seating, holding the wheel correctly, trailing the brakes into the apex, accelerating, straightening the path of the car, and setting up for the next turn—is the ultimate enjoyment of motoring and certainly the ultimate skill of road racing.

There is another "driving task" to be added to the high-performance bag of skills: gearshifting. We have no idea how many drivers on the road today don't have any notion about shifting and declutching or how many have not had to do either for so long that they have lost their mechanical skill with a gearshift and a clutch. The statistics must be astounding. Except for a few sports car and drag racing buffs, very few drivers order their cars with manual transmissions and stickshifts any more.

Race cars, with few exceptions, have manual transmissions. Road racing machines have four, five, and six forward speeds. To get the benefit of maximum torque exiting the corners, it is commonly desirable to downshift while braking and turning. The coordinated combination of movements which produce downshifting, braking, turning, light braking, acceleration, and upshifting is the total package that adds to the enjoyment of performance motoring.

Race driving conditions also call for a technique called "heel and toeing," which provides for the operation of three pedals with two feet. While the left foot is busy with the clutch, the right foot is shared between the brake and the accelerator. With practice, it is easy to hold the brake lightly with the ball of the right foot and swing the heel over to press on the gas pedal. "Heel and toeing" takes a little practice, because it is not one of the readily taught skills of driving, but it is easier to do than it sounds.

High-performance driving also requires learning and perfecting a technique more commonly associated with truck driving called double clutching, which is used more often during downshifting. While shifting, the driver pauses in neutral, lets out the clutch pedal, then pushes it in again and drops to the lower gear (or upshifts). When downshifting, the driver blips the throttle during the pause at neutral, using the heel-and-toe technique so as not to get the car off balance, and brings the engine revolutions up to synchronize with drive train speed so the gears can mesh quietly and smoothly.

The image of race drivers shoving gears into position, whipping the wheel around, and diving into corners simply isn't correct. Smoothness is the most important single attribute of a successful competitor. In fact, the best driver usually doesn't look like he is going as fast as he is. His smoothness makes it appear as though he isn't trying as hard as the others on the track.

None of the skills of the high-performance driver are impossible to learn for a person in unimpaired physical condition. To the average driver, they're not as easy as they sound, but they are not difficult to master with a proper amount of practice. Putting them all together requires something else to an extraordinary degree: concentration.

Since graduating from the Bondurant school, the writer has learned to respect the professional golfer who can study the thirty-foot putt, knowing that a nationwide TV audience is watching, and then walk over and knock the ball in the hole. He has learned to admire the quarterback who can stand in the pocket with violence all around him, waiting to get clotheslined, and calmly deliver the football to a player running an erratic pattern thirty yards downfield. They have that one common asset, concentration, but they don't have to make use of it over such long periods as the race driver does. A moment's loss of concentration isn't nearly as dangerous for anyone as it is for a race driver.

Concentration at the wheel of a racing machine at the Bob Bondurant school is difficult to describe, because I had never had to deal with it at that level before. The best I can do is to relate it to conditions that week. There was a heat wave. On Monday temperatures climbed into the high 90s, and by Friday the thermometer read 115 in the shade, but there was no shade on Ontario's blistering infield. Heat inside the car itself was almost enough to blister the bottoms of your feet, but I didn't even feel the heat while running the car at speed, only when I stopped and got out.

I used to think of concentration as something you used when you shut out the radio or crowd noise while writing a story for the newspaper. Or trying to remember something to answer a question on an exam. Or coming up with a person's name when he popped up in a crowd.

Concentration in this case means withdrawing all your senses and rationing them out to the job of driving that automobile. It was almost an eerie feeling, like being shut up in a room, away from the rest of the world. Time meant nothing, only driving. Somehow I knew when I was doing one thing right and another wrong, knew it while I was doing it, and I would talk silently to myself, telling myself to remember what I had done wrong when I came around next time so I would do it right.

The difference between the attitude of the average motorist and the student in the Bondurant school toward driving is nearly impossible to describe. I can't think of any other activity that requires as much concentration as driving a race car.

If a motorist on the street were to cultivate one-tenth of this degree of concentration, there would be only one-third as many accidents on the highways as there are. Richard Spear, who heads the federal government's National Transportation Safety Bureau as general manager, pointed out that scheduled aviation contributes something like 300 accidental deaths a year, whereas the annual highway toll is 54,000.

"It looks like we are spending our safety money all wrong," he said. "We put it all into aviation, when the problem lies somewhere else."

We could learn from the aviation industry, which sets up elaborate licensing procedures and also polices its pilots far more effectively than highway traffic authorities do. If administrators like Mr. Spear have much to say about it, a lot of flying safety practices may be adapted to the road in the years ahead.

It is standard procedure, for instance, for the pilot to check out every instrument and control in his cockpit after walking around the craft and carefully checking out everything on the outside of the airplane. For cross-country flights he will file a flight plan. To get his license, he not only has to demonstrate his ability to control the craft, but his knowledge of navigation as well. His license is restricted to aircraft of certain size and power, and he keeps a log that shows how many hours of experience he has accumulated. To fly on instruments he must have a special license, and to keep that license active he must fly a minimum number of hours each year on instruments to demonstrate that he is staying in practice.

Imagine that you were to operate a car the way a commercial pilot flies his plane. The Federal Aviation Agency prescribes a certain preflight sequence of checkoffs, the make of the plane dictates others, and each airline adds to that list its own requirements. A United Air Lines Boeing 727 flight crew has a total of 208 steps it must go through before takeoff and another 86 chores that must be done individually or as a team by the pilot, co-pilot, flight engineer, and navigator every time one of its airliners leaves the terminal. Every flying officer must have this list of procedures memorized so well that he can recite it any time an FAA examiner asks him.

In practice, all racing drivers go through what amounts to a "preflight check" before taking their cars out onto the track. Of course, they have plenty of professional help. In some cases they even do major engine repairs between runs on the race track. The drivers themselves do their own preflights, carefully walking around the car to inspect the work done by mechanics, questioning them about ride heights and tire pressures, looking at parts that had been removed and replaced to see that they are properly buttoned in again.

Once in the cockpit and belted securely in place, the professional race driver instinctively works the controls and scans the instruments. He keeps watch on the tachometer as engine oil is warmed up, and his gauges are a lot more critical than those found in the ordinary street machine—oil temperature and pressure, fuel supply and pressure, rev counter (tachometer). It's the rare race car that has a speedometer, because miles an hour are a meaningless readout to a driver on the track. He doesn't have to worry about speed limits. He is concerned with two things only: winning and safety, and not always necessarily in that order.

By contrast, most street drivers tend to jump in their cars, turn on the key, and go. The professional, the knowledgeable, and the high-performance drivers don't do that.

So let's check out the family sedan the right way.

With most modern automobiles it isn't necessary to check the oil and water levels every day, but it wouldn't be foolish to lift the hood and periodically check battery, battery cables, water, oil, brake and automatic system fluids, hoses, wiring harnesses, spark plug wires, and belts.

If one would approach his car every morning the way airline pilots do, the first thing would be a visual inspection trip around the car. Are the tires low? Have any nicks appeared in the body overnight from the previous day's running? Are there any rust spots to note for correction in the near future? Are there telltale signs of leaking oil, fuel, or water under the car? Are hang-ons such as the license plates, hub caps, outside rear-view mirror, and radio antenna in place? How are things under the hood?

Climbing into the driver's seat and buckling up—that would include a shoulder harness as well as a lap belt, as far as any serious high-performance driver is concerned—one would automatically go over a routine checklist that might be like this:

1) Secure all doors and windows, locking doors.

2) Check seat position.

3) Check rear-view mirrors.

4) Check hand brake.

5) Check fuel level.

6) Start engine. Maintain low and even revs, high enough to prevent stallout. Depending on air temperature, engine warmup should normally take from thirty seconds to two minutes.

7) Try brakes and steering.

8) Scan instruments—alternator, oil pressure, and water temperature gauges—to see if the readings are normal. (Many American cars indicate positive charge and safe oil pressure only with red lights which come on when charge and oil are not correct. If you are serious about maintaining a high-performance car, add the appropriate instruments to your dash. They can be purchased at dealerships, auto supply stores, and speed shops, even at some discount stores' automotive service departments.)

9) Check out turn signal indicators. At night check out headlights, taillights, and backup lights by getting out of the car if necessary and walking around it again.

The automobile is a very forgiving piece of equipment. It runs, that is it carries its occupants, on as little as 40 percent efficiency at times. Some of the smoking, mangled, noisy, wobbly wrecks that are driven daily on the expressways operate on three of their eight cylinders, the other five having expired due to lack of care, lack of interest, lack of money, or a combination of all three.

Up to now we have discussed the principles and the mechanics of high-performance driving. To master these it is necessary to practice, to apply understanding of vehicle dynamics to how a car responds. No amount of reading will give you the feel of acceleration from 0 to 60 or trying to corner at a rapid rate of speed as well as practice with a car.

The ideal way would be to go through all the maneuvers with a professional racing-wise instructor at your side. If you can't do that, however, try to follow these three tips by Bondurant:

1) Be smooth.
2) *Be Smooth.*
3) *BE SMOOTH!*

That means smooth braking, gradually increasing foot pressure on the brakes, not hard stabbing or on and off braking. That means trailing the brakes to keep the nose of the car down in the corners until it is time to accelerate out.

Being smooth means don't jam the accelerator to the floor, but increase the throttle in a smooth motion. De-clutch smoothly. Turn the wheel smoothly. Make no quick motions at all. The smoother you are, the faster you go.

Let's have a word about speed. On the road course speed means lap times, not high velocity between any two intermediate points. On the street speed means efficiency, not how fast the car will go wide open on the freeway. Overall, average speed is important on the street as well as the track, because, after all, an automobile is a transportation system. If it were not important to go fast, we might be content to ride around in hay wagons pulled by plow horses. The federal government spends billions building high-speed highways so we can move faster around the country, to make our automobile travel more efficient. Safety should not be an end in itself but a by-product of efficiency. The definition of high-performance driving should be the operating of a vehicle at its maximum capability with safety.

The winning race driver may prove his courage, mechanical knowledge, ability to communicate with his crew, and confidence in himself, but more importantly he proves his efficiency in controlling a vehicle. On a race track smoothness wins.

On the street smoothness gets a driver where he is going quickest with the least possible fuss. The smooth driver doesn't collect traffic citations, and he doesn't have accidents. He doesn't do unpredictable things on the street and cause other motorists to have accidents. In emergency situations he almost always does the right thing automatically. Why? Smoothness gives him an advantage over other drivers, who are hung out and fighting for control more often than not at those critical times. It's great to have the lightning reflexes that give a driver fast reaction time, but without smoothness and the sense of what to do in an emergency, those reactions are no help at all.

3

The Tactics of Driving

Driving on a race track is a precise art, but no one style of driving an automobile on the public roads is correct to the exclusion of all others. Even the pros differ in their approaches to driving the expressways and city streets.

The high-performance objective, remember, is to get there quickest with the least amount of trouble, including legal complications. In most cases that implies obeying speed laws. Ask any race driver and he will launch into his three-minute speech on traffic safety, which is built around the theme: "I get all the speed thrills I need on the race track. When I'm on the street, I slow down and obey all the traffic regulations."

That's a worthy comment, something that would look good on a National Safety Council billboard, but in practice it's a different story. For one thing, racing crews are in the habit of speeding from track to track with their trucks and trailers, driving night and day through all sorts of weather. If they're not late getting started because of something that had to be done to the race car, they're in a hurry to get to the next race anyway so they can start working on it as soon as possible. The stories of cross-country races by the racing fraternity are legendary. In most cases, a lot of the driving is done by those same "slow down on the street" race drivers. The top pros don't have to live the same gypsy existence their mechanics do, because they usually fly into the site of an upcoming event. But they do put a lot of miles on their personal wheels or rental cars when they are away from home pursuing their livelihood, which is much of the time.

Most professional drivers confess a little edginess about two-way traffic on city streets and country roads, because auto racing is done in one direction at a time. Their concern on the street is not so much their own ability or the condition of the vehicle they are driving, but the unpredictability of other motorists on the street with them.

It's understandable that Bobby Allison might become a little nervous coping with unfamiliar Los Angeles freeways. On the big tracks, he is confronted with the same skillful professionals week after week. He knows what to expect from Richard Petty, Bobby Isaac, David Pearson, Buddy Baker, and other drivers he sees at least thirty times a year.

The most thoughtful and practical driver of all in his public statements on highway safety is Richard Petty, the acknowledged all-time champion of stock car racing. Petty deliberately breaks the speed limits in his home state of North Carolina to keep himself more alert. He claims it forces him to refer continually to his rear-view mirror in search of the telltale signs of a traffic officer. If he were to obey the conservative speed limits on many of the open highways in his home state, he claims, he would get careless from the lack of challenge and let his mind wander.

Petty doesn't endorse breaking the law and doesn't recommend that every motorist drive five or ten miles an hour over the speed limit in order to sharpen his concentration. He is merely honest about how he copes with a problem common to most of us. He enjoys driving up to the capabilities of car and driver. Moreover, he feels compelled to do so. If the car is safe, the road is clear, and the driver is alert, the Petty reasoning goes, he is better off to sharpen his own senses by driving in a high-performance mode than he is to poke along at quite a bit less than his own abilities. As we pointed out before, an automobile is a transportation system. The capacity of both car and driver is wasted when it is operated at less than safe total efficiency.

The controversial opinions of Richard Petty do not confine themselves to posted speed limits. If he had his way, there would be no automobile insurance. Petty believes that if every driver on the road had to pay for the damage he causes in an accident, there would be fewer accidents.

"Look at all these people driving up on the bumpers of the cars in front of them," Petty observed while riding as a passenger down Wilshire Boulevard in Los Angeles. "If there were no auto insurance, they'd be staying a half a block apart. They would sure be a lot more careful than they are now."

Petty's expertise with a stock car is well known. A lesser celebrity, now retired as an active road racing competitor, is Miles Gupton, who has another unique strategy on the freeways and city streets where he has driven an average of 50,000 miles annually for thirty years. Gupton's accident record is almost spotless. He was asked once how he did it.

"I get the chance to have an accident about twice a day," he said. "The trick is to stay out of the way of the idiots. I've been up in the ivy [that borders the freeway] getting out of the way, and I've been up on the center divider, but I've never been into another car."

He had one traffic accident in 1947.

"A guy ran a signal and hit me in the back end, because I just couldn't get out of the way."

Despite his safety record, Gupton pays high insurance rates, because he collects more than his share of traffic tickets.

"I drive fast, and I am naturally more exposed to tickets than others because of the miles I cover," he said, without a trace of bitterness toward traffic officers. "Police have to concentrate on speeders and reckless drivers, simply because there are so many cars on the road they can't concentrate on the real cause of most accidents, the inept driver.

"This idiot may not break any laws, but he is a menace just the same. He can't be counted on to do the right thing, the expected thing, in an emergency. He can be counted on to drive unconsciously, over his head, and sloppily."

How Gupton survives his frequent encounters with "idiots" is to keep his foot off the brakes. He explains that he would rather be in motion when somebody else is on a collision course with him.

As Gupton points out, most everything that is done in an automobile on the street has to do with traffic around the car. That includes other cars, trucks, motorcycles, trains, buses, pedestrians, and even animals and impediments that roll onto the traffic lanes, such as rocks, tumbleweeds, and pieces that fall off of other vehicles.

Coping with traffic is what driving is all about, on the track and on the street. In either context, good high-performance driving is the highest form of safe driving. Let's take up what can be done to survive while driving for enjoyment on the street.

1) *Develop alertness.* A high-performance driver takes pride in what he is doing behind the wheel, while the great majority of other motorists perform in robot-like fashion.

Let's face it. If you don't care any more for a motor vehicle than for the fact that it carries you from where you are to where you want to go, the functions of driving can get to be rather routine. The modern zombie at the wheel can't concentrate on driving, because he believes it is too simple a task. There are a lot of things about today's automobile that reinforce this notion. First, there are the automatic systems, which reduce the number of functions he has to perform and which take the physical labor out of steering and braking. The ultimate of these is cruise control; with it the driver doesn't even need to touch his gas pedal. Second, there is the soft, quiet, comfortable ride, which creates a relaxing atmosphere inside the cockpit of many large and intermediate size sedans. Third, there are the diversions available to the driver, such as the car radio, cigarette lighter, and stereo system. Fourth, for the driver who wants to shut himself off completely from the environment there are heaters, air conditioners, and insulated bodies (which wipe out all engine noises and most outside noises as well—including, regrettably, the sirens of emergency vehicles). Fifth, and most important, is the driver's own lack of awareness that driving is a skill that must be developed, and that staying out of the way of other drivers is a heavy responsibility.

The quickest way to know your alterness is lagging is when your car wanders out of its proper lane. On many modern freeways and expressways small buttons have been built into the lane markings so that you immediately hear from your tires when you run over them. Take one hand off the wheel to light a cigarette, and you hear the telltale thump-thump-thump underneath the car. Another danger sign easy to recognize: You have forgotten exactly where you are or where you are going. When that happens, you had better jog your mind, start looking for street or highway signs, and get your act together. You've been daydreaming.

Altertness means more than staying awake. It means being aware of what the other drivers are doing around you. Are oncoming cars flashing their high beams at you? Check yours. Is anybody acting strangely near you? He might be drunk or sleepy or on dope or getting sick. Be extra careful of him. Is the guy next to you or in front or in back of you taking his eyes off the road to talk to his passenger? Keep track of him. He could ram you in an instant, or, if he is in front, get disoriented and slam on his brakes for no logical reason. Are there optical illusions on the road that seem to menace you? Glare can hide obstacles in the road or eliminate all forward vision for long periods of time. A shadow across the road could conceal a small child or a dog or a large rock. You need to anticipate any unusual sight up ahead so that it doesn't surprise you when it pops up a few feet away.

2) *Second-guess the other drivers.* Learn the signs that tell you what another driver is thinking or doing.

If a car ahead is crowding the left side of his lane, he may be about to do one of several things without signaling. Get ready for him. He may change from the right to the left lane, but then again, he may be getting ready for a right-hand turn. Or he may be absent-mindedly drifting to the left and could make an abrupt correction. How do you know what he is planning? What is he thinking about? How alert is he? You can tell a lot by observing the way he operates his car and what movements he makes with his head and his arms.

If he looks into the rear-view mirror repeatedly or glances back over his left shoulder, you can bet he is about to switch lanes to the left. If he looks back over his right shoulder, he is probably getting ready to change lanes to the right. If he looks ahead to the left, he is probably going to turn right; he's looking for the cross traffic. When he turns his head he might not look all the way around but sneak furtive glances to right or left. If that is the case, look out. He is about ready to change lanes without warning and may cut too close in front of the trailing car in that lane. That car might be yours.

You can bet the driver is not paying attention when the car wanders to the right or left and he doesn't seem to make any head movements at all. Sometimes the head movements become exaggerated, and those are danger signs. He might be getting drowsy, or he might be exhausted. Worse yet, he might be intoxicated.

Keep an eye out for the man who reaches back with a free hand and rubs his neck. He's tired. He may be fighting the desire to shut his eyes and go to sleep. He may be the victim of a mild form of epilepsy called ataxia, which imitates drowsiness and is believed to cause many of the "falling asleep at the wheel" auto accident deaths. Carbon monoxide fumes may be leaking through the floorboards of his car and poisoning him, causing drowsiness. In extreme cases, the sleepy driver will gradually lower his head. If he is lucky, he will awaken before disaster overtakes him, and in that case you will see his head bob upright again, only to lower slowly once more as he continues to drift off.

A driver's head gives him away in other situations as well. If the roadway suddenly becomes blocked, and the driver of the car in front of you shows no reaction with his head, shoulders, or arms, you don't have to look at his brake lights to know he is slow to react and will momentarily go into a panic stop.

Be careful when you are behind a compulsive talker, especially one who uses his hands a lot in conversation. That is a danger signal that tells a lot. Talking with a passenger is a minor diversion, not especially harmful to the driver's performance. The chances are good, however, that the driver is talking while listening to the car radio at the same time, dragging his attention away from the road in separate directions. Many people also find it difficult to talk without looking at the other party in the conversation. So the talker turns his head to face the listener. If he looks away from the road ahead of him for one second at sixty miles an hour, he will travel 88 feet literally blind, with neither the perception of where he is nor the memory of where he has been. Add to the equation the use of hands to dramatize what he is talking about. Most people who drive, talk, and wave their arms will keep one hand on the wheel. There is an unconscious movement of the wheel hand, however, in sympathy with the free hand. Usually it's just a twitch, not significant. But at freeway speeds a twitch is sometimes all that is necessary to put a motorist into a panic situation. Stay well behind hand talkers, and when passing them, get out of their way, give them lots of room.

The complete slob will take both hands off the wheel when talking, and he is a menace to everyone on the roadway. First he lifts both hands off the steering wheel to talk, diverting his attention from driving and drastically reducing his control over the car. If something happens to make him recover his senses and drop his hands back to the wheel, that very act could force him out of control. If he is in the habit of taking both hands off the wheel, he'll get good at it and may not veer too far off a straight line. But if he catches himself by surprise, watch out. He could be all over the road in an instant. On a two-way street this is particularly hazardous for obvious reasons. The motorist lighting a cigarette or a pipe isn't normally a worry, because he is usually well practiced and if he uses his car lighter doesn't have to take his eyes off the road to see what he is doing for more than the instant he raises the lighter to the end of his cigarette. Look out, however, for the fumbler, the guy who can't find his pack of fags or his matches, who has to grope for the lighter or knock off burning pieces of tobacco into the ashtray or look down to see where he accidentally dropped his burning match or cigarette.

3) *Stay out of the way of aggressors.* You can't cure the world's mental illnesses from behind the wheel of your own automobile, but you can keep yourself from agitating a vicious drunk or a lunatic. I got into one of those situations once, and it wasn't too pleasant.

Driving the pace car for a road race from Los Angeles International Airport to a newspaper office downtown, with another reporter and a photographer as passengers, I didn't notice this glazed-eye fellow leering at the huge letters painted on the side of our borrowed new "super car." This was one of the first Pontiac Grand Prix ever seen on the street, and it was bright red. With lettering on the side it was very conspicuous in traffic.

Our car stepped out briskly at each signal eastbound on Century Boulevard, heading toward the Harbor Freeway, which leads to the downtown area. I didn't even know the fellow was around, which was mistake number one. It was nighttime, and we might not have been able to see him too well anyway, teeth clenched and hunched over the steering wheel of a battered, smoking, almost unpainted automobile that could only be loosely termed a "transportation car."

I entered the freeway northbound at normal speed. There was practically no traffic in either direction. Suddenly, here came the klunker, whizzing by so close that he almost scraped paint off the left side of the Pontiac. Once past us he pulled over into our lane and slowed down. Thinking he was merely having some mechanical trouble I passed him, still not aware that something more serious was the matter. Again he passed, this time on the right side, and he pulled in front of us. He slowed almost to a crawl as we came over a rise, and I started to scan the rear-view mirror to see if anybody was coming up fast enough behind to endanger us. I made an instant decision—shake this clown.

"Hang on," I said, and we peeled off to the right onto an off-ramp at 37th Street. One quick turn into an empty parking lot and out the other side, and we were on the Exposition Boulevard on-ramp heading once again for downtown Los Angeles on the freeway. I looked back, and there was no sign of the other car. We slowed from 75 to a normal 55 and began merging into the right-hand lanes that led to the downtown off-ramps.

Suddenly there he was again, on our left, scowling wickedly. That's when we saw the bottle of booze. It was a pint, wrapped in a brown paper bag. He started edging over on us. The situation had been bad up to that point, but now it was survival. It was easy to see he was trying to force us into the overpass abutment at 7th Street or 6th Street. We didn't know if he had any weapons in his car. We now had a race on our hands, to stay ahead of him in order to reach the 4th Street off-ramp in one piece.

The 4th Street off-ramp is a hairpin 90-degree right-hand uphill turn leading to a four-lane one-way street.

About a quarter mile east on 4th Street, the road dives downhill into the main part of the city, where there is a stop signal at every intersection. The first street we came to was Olive Avenue; a rapid conference with my two passengers, and a joint decision was reached to lead this insane fool right back to the company parking lot at 2nd and Broadway—unless we could shake him by making an unexpected left turn at Olive. By this time he was two lanes over to our right, and it looked as if he was trying to get alongside of us so he could batter us.

We made a quick left on Olive, but he was wider—in a better "line" than we were—and he had apparently anticipated what we were trying to do, because he got around in better shape than we did. The hill we were climbing on Olive took its toll on his tired and overworked engine, however, and as we zipped up toward 3rd Street he was dropping back. Fortunately, there were no pedestrians crossing the street from the top of Angels Flight as there usually were at that hour. We roared up to 1st Street, over to Broadway and into the lot, using a hidden entrance. The pursuer turned into the main driveway and came clanking to a stop against the chain that blocked the driveway. He hadn't even seen the chain. Three very angry and frightened newspapermen held him (our photographer had a gun in his car, which he produced) until the police arrived.

If it sounds like getting involved with a murderous lunatic on the public roads is a neat adventure, don't you believe it. There is no fun to it. The best "medicine" is preventive—stay out of the way of kooks, drunks, and loonies.

Don't race them. Don't defy them. Don't try to "teach them a lesson." Be as inconspicuous as possible, and if you have to run away, go in the direction of the nearest police station. In our case, we were looking desperately for a policeman. Not finding one, we did the next best thing—we made a beeline for the photographer's car, which not only had a gun inside, but had a radio that enabled us to talk to the city desk of the newspaper, where a hotline was connected to the police reporter, one room removed from the Los Angeles Police Department's radio dispatchers.

It's also good to remember where law officers are likely to be found, in case you need one in a hurry. In my end of the small beach town where I live, there is a hot dog stand where officers hang out during their breaks. In case of any trouble, I'd head there. Even if there were no police cars parked outside, the chances are the cafe owner would know how to summon help more quickly than other ordinary citizens.

Chances are you will go through life without ever encountering a dangerously demented motorist or one crazed with alcohol and belligerency. The more typical aggressors you will meet are the selfish drivers who cut you off (sometimes unconsciously, but occasionally to satisfy some aggressive craving in their psyche), the red light bandits who speed through an intersection just as you get the green "go" signal, and the frustrated "Snakes" and "Mongooses" who can't resist the temptation to treat every signal light like a drag strip Christmas tree.

Another worrisome type is the tailgater. It's impossible to cope with the motorist who insists on driving too close to your rear bumper. Let him get by. Don't play games with him. I confess to having done that, and I'm not particularly proud of myself. Unfortunately, hitting the gas and the brakes at the same time to scare him doesn't work; it only makes him mad to be thrown out of control deliberately.

Tailgaters are sometimes unconscious souls, and anybody who doesn't know exactly where he is in relation to the other traffic is not to be trusted. More often than not, however, tailgaters are aggressive drivers who are pushing you, "suggesting" that you move over and let them by. Psychologists who have studied the deep meanings of these things claim that two emotions are expressed by the tailgater and tailgatee, both of which could be termed aggressive. The tailgater is goading the driver in front by "intruding" on his personal space, while the crowded motorist resents this intrusion. Space is defined as that area around every person that is his subconscious protective shield, his inviolate territory. If that psychological theory is correct, we are all subject to aggressive feelings when somebody gets too close to us in traffic, but we are also better off knowing why we feel that way. In other words, let the tailgater push you around. Move over and let him by. That's a basic law of survival on the public roads, although on the race track it doesn't always necessarily apply.

4) *Think ahead.* Merely knowing what is going on around you and having the ability to anticipate and react to changing traffic conditions isn't enough. The skill of thinking your way from place to place is as much a part

of high-performance driving as avoiding accidents and executing perfect maneuvers.

One of the great underground motoring events of our day is the Cannonball Baker Sea-to-Shining-Sea Memorial Trophy Dash, a non-sanctioned, illegal race over public highways from New York City to Redondo Beach, California, by a group of enthusiasts, writers, press agents, and race drivers. The first time it was held, in 1971, Dan Gurney and Brock Yates won it in a Ferrari. The next year three relatively unknown road racing enthusiasts won it in a stock Cadillac. The ultimate weapon in each case was not a tricky suspension system or a high revving engine, but a good road map combined with careful planning.

The winners simply took the fastest routes with the fewest hazards and least number of possible delays. While some of the competitors built trick fuel storage systems into their machines so they could cut down on the number of gas stops and others practiced deceptions to avoid arrests, the '73 Cadillac team of Steve Behr, Bill Canfield, and Fred Olds covered 2,940 miles in 37 hours, 16 minutes, an average of 78.8 miles per hour including stops, merely by driving smoothly and unobtrusively along a carefully plotted course.

Federal highway safety authorities don't spout the statistics, but they claim a significant number of accidents are caused by confusion over highway signs, street markings, and road geometry. Nowhere in the safety or driving literature, except in books and magazines read almost exclusively by highway engineers, can you find the explanation for interstate highway numbering systems or road sign placement. Yet, armed with that knowledge and thereby able to decode the secret numbering systems used by highway engineers, a driver would be a lot better prepared to cope with the freeway environment and could possibly estimate just where he is in the United States.

Even-numbered interstates, for instance, are east-west throughways. The southernmost, I-4, connects St. Petersburg with Daytona Beach. I-10 leads from Los Angeles through Phoenix, El Paso, Houston, New Orleans, and Mobile to Jacksonville. The farther north you go in the country, the higher the east-west interstate route number. I-90, for instance, leads from Seattle through Butte, Sioux Falls, Madison, Chicago, Cleveland, Buffalo, and Syracuse to Boston.

Odd-numbered interstates are north-south routes. I-5 connects San Diego with Seattle, via Los Angeles, San Francisco, and Portland. I-35 stretches from Laredo, Texas, to Duluth, Minnesota, through Dallas, Oklahoma City, Kansas City, Des Moines, and St. Paul. I-95 is the easternmost of the interstate chain, leading northward from Miami through Fayetteville, Richmond, Washington, Baltimore, New York, Providence, and Boston to Houlton, Maine. In other words, the higher the number the farther east you are.

The important thing to understand about highway and freeway signs is that their logic is perfectly clear only to the highway engineer. None of the intricate coding that appears on signs along the road has ever been properly explained to the motoring public. So admits Jerry Alexander, a brilliant young engineer with the Department of Transportation, in this interview:

Q: What are the mistakes typical of drivers who misread signs along the highway?

A: There is a concept called "driver expectancy." People in general have expectancies about everything in their daily lives, and particularly about driving, about what their car will do, because it's always done it. Putting your foot on the brake with a certain force, you expect the car to slow at a rate it has always slowed at that force. They also expect certain things of signs and markings. There is a little old lady from Dubuque who is going to take a trip to L.A. She expects to find a sign to Los Angeles as soon as she gets out on the freeway. A lot of these expectancies are immature or naïve, but people have them nevertheless. It's logical from their point of view that they have them, because there is no way of knowing what there is going to be a sign for on the highway. There is a fair assumption that there are signs, so it's a fair assumption that the place I'm going to is going to be signed for.

My orientation is not so much the driver, but to tell the highway engineers what the driver's orientation is, so that he can design a signing system or a road marking system or something most responsive to what the driver thinks he is going to get. To turn that around and tell drivers what highway engineers are giving them is an extremely difficult thing to do. More often than not, highway engineers don't know what they are giving them. It is never the same twice. I don't get many arguments from highway engineers on that. They say, we follow the manual on traffic control devices. That's the Bible on all traffic devices.

There is a method to the madness of highway marking and signing. Unfortunately, most people don't know it. While we talk a lot about signing uniformity, there are many places where there is no uniformity. We suffer because of it. There are so many things drivers expect and don't get. Signing is one. For example, coming into the Washington, D.C., area, you might expect a sign for Silver Spring, but you won't see it. A driver who is coming in from Chicago to Silver Spring will say, "Okay, when I hit I-70S, I'll see a sign for it." It's just not there. So it puts him in a vulnerable position. How is he going to get where he is going? While that is not directly related to staying alive, indirectly it is, because when you spend so much time looking for a sign, the likelihood is that you are going to miss more important information, like where the road is going, where the cars are going.

Q: Are there any statistics on accidents caused by bad sign development?

A: There are very few studies I know of that tie accidents down to bad signing. The House Congressional Committee on Roads has looked at the problem. They've taken films to show the erratic maneuvers at intersections. They've estimated something like six to nine percent of the drivers in any interchange are likely to become confused, either by the signing or the geometry of the roadway. While there are few data to tie accidents to bad signing, there are very strong gut feelings that this is the case. You get people doing a lot of stupid things because they don't understand the signs. They'll go halfway up a ramp and back down and can cause a tremendous collision. The percentages of traffic irregularities are very small, but when you consider the total numbers involved, it's mind boggling. It really is.

We use a lot of different codings on the highway system that have a meaning for us but little if any for the driver. Like the numbering systems on the interstates. A lot of these little codes—you can say that's good, that's neat. For example, you have a cloverleaf interchange, and the advance notification reads, "Exits 1 Mile," plural. That letter *s* is a code that says there are two ramps there, not one. That's the only information you get. The drivers don't know that. If they knew, they might be in a better position to take the correct ramp. There are an awful lot of little things like that. We don't really—when I say *we* I don't mean the Federal Highway Commission, I'm talking about the whole damn highway community—bother to explain to the motoring public.

Alexander claims that many highway engineers don't even realize there is confusion over the codes they use to mark the federal highway system. He stated, "They look at me and say, 'Gee, didn't you know that?' " Other "secret" codes exist to help the hip motorist. One is the mileage sign. Federal highways must have a mileage sign every five miles.

"There is a sequence when you come to an interstate," Alexander explained. "You have a requirement to have a speed limit, to have a route confirmation marker, to have a mileage sign. The bottom line of that mileage sign has to have the name of the control city. Control cities—there's not much on what they are—but they are essentially the major cities that can be reached on that route. That control city has to be repeated on every mileage sign until it is reached, at which time the next control city is listed.

"You can have a mileage sign of two destinations or three. The control city has to be on the route itself. In other words, if you are on I-95 going south from Washington, the control city is Richmond, right on the route. The top listing is an intermediate destination which is also on the route. You can have a middle destination on the sign, which does not have to be on the route. It needs to be accessible from the route. But it doesn't remain the same until it is passed, you can alternate in that middle line. There is a method to that madness also. You won't find signs after every interchange if the interchanges are spaced closer than every five miles. That's a code, but I wouldn't be able to articulate that code to you. It's just something that's hidden away in the back.

"We have a lot of difficulties with control cities. For example, there are several locations around the country where you'll have two adjacent states with a large city adjacent to each other, like Council Bluffs, Iowa, and Omaha, Nebraska. When it comes to identifying control cities, we have trouble. They are both large towns. Which do you sign for? It turns out that states can get to play a game of chicken with each other. Iowa says, 'To hell with you. We're not going to sign for Omaha.' Nebraska says, 'If you're not going to sign for Omaha, we're not going to sign for Council Bluffs.' That's the kind of silliness that goes on, and we don't have any control over it. In highway programs there is an awful lot of state's rights and state politics involved. I guess you can imagine that. While we hold a very large purse string, the politics involved negate the effectiveness of that purse string as a cudgel."

C. F. Scheffy, another Federal Highway Administration official, concedes signs and intersections are confusing to the average motorist for still other reasons.

"There are two types of problems with drivers," he said. "One, the confusion because the driver is not getting the message about his route—it is coming at him too fast or it isn't properly oriented. The other is that drivers are unaware of how certain things in the interchange are intended to function. There are many drivers who will not use an acceleration ramp properly but will drive up a ramp and stop right at the point where they should be at merging speed. In the cloverleaf there is a conflict system where we use the same roadway both for accelerating traffic coming on and also for the decelerating traffic coming off. It is one of the reasons that the cloverleaf is being dispensed with in high-speed highways.

"Awareness of drivers as to how these features are intended to function is one of the big gaps in driver education right now. There is a gap between the features which the highway designer has built into the highway to make it safer and the driver's understanding of how he is supposed to use [them]. It's not the driver's fault. It's a failure to communicate."

All this means that you should be well prepared to travel from Point A to Point B in your automobile, both in terms of the route you want to travel, road conditions to be encountered, traffic problems, "pit stops," freeway exits, entrances, and interchanges. In the case of travel over unfamiliar roads, remember the universal rule of good sense: Don't overdrive what can be seen on the road ahead.

I have driven through, over, and around the maze of Los Angeles and vicinity for nearly thirty years and consider myself well oriented. None of the major streets in Los Angeles and Orange County are unfamiliar to me. Yet I hate to venture out in that environment without taking along a *Thomas Bros. Street Guide*. It's a map book, and there are others like it which may or may not be better. Map books are far superior to road maps that fold open. A map book can be balanced on the steering wheel if necessary and scanned quickly, but it is best used in tracing a route from Point A to Point B before starting out. That fixes the drive in your mind and suggests all the alternatives, in case the traffic gets too heavy.

Long-distance driving invariably leads you to strange cities; you will find that practicing a conscious effort to zero in on your destinations will soon give you a sort of sixth sense. You will be able to drive into the heart of nearly any city and quickly find city hall or the county courthouse, the local newspaper office, the hospital, the central plaza or park. In the outskirts you will know exactly where to find motel row. Most large American cities have a pattern—here we put the industrial district, there the apartments, there the business district—that is violated only in isolated cases. Small towns in the plains particularly have a sameness to them, right down to the location of speed traps, and the architecture is almost always sure to give away the identity of the region.

To know where you are and how to get where you're going may seem too simple-minded an instruction to give serious attention, but remember what the government says, six to nine percent of all accidents are caused by confusion over road signing or road geometry. That's an impressive statistic. It's also a subject they don't cover in driver education.

4

Accidents Can Happen

The American College Dictionary states that an accident is an "undesirable or unfortunate happening" that occurs "unexpectedly, without design, or by chance." Traffic accidents have been with us as long as traffic has, but it's more serious to get run over by a car in the twentieth century than it was by a horse in the nineteenth. If you believe the theories of probability, you must subscribe to the notion that the more cars and trucks there are on the road, the higher the accident rate has to go, rising by geometric progression rather than by simple one plus one arithmetic progression.

In other words, if all but one motorist in the United States parked his car and only that one motorist ventured out on the empty streets, the chances of his having an accident would be exceedingly small. If a second car was backed out of its garage, those chances would more than double, because there is always the possibility that the second motorist would run into the first, or vice versa. Multiply this mythical example into reality, and you arrive at today's situation—100 million motor vehicles in operation every day, 10,000 injuries daily, 54,000 deaths a year, and $10 billion in annual losses from 800,000 traffic accidents. Since 1900 there have been two million deaths from motor vehicle accidents, more persons killed "unexpectedly, without design, or by chance" than on purpose by all the wars in this century.

Obviously, so many deaths and injuries and so much waste of our resources have drawn the attention of behavioral scientists. By and large, they are pretty levelheaded and cool about the whole thing. They understand things like probability. They do what we all ought to do—they *accept* accidents. Accidents are a statistical reality, and no amount of "speed kills!" propaganda is going to change that fact.

One school of thought in the safety business says that officials should stop wasting so much time, money, and energy trying to prevent accidents, and start making motor vehicles safer to crash in. The leading argument for this theory is that attempts to influence driver behavior through propaganda, enforcement of traffic laws, driver education and retraining, license revocation penalties, and publicity of the gory details of fatal accidents have all failed miserably to curb the spiraling death rate. There is some validity in this point of view. A great deal of opportunity to improve the safety of motor vehicles had been overlooked until the safety crusaders and the federal government began making everyone aware of the situation. The crashable car is almost a symbol of the consumer movement of the '70s, a movement generated by Ralph Nader. Nader has gone on to other fields, but in his wake he left behind a huge government bureacracy dedicated to forcing crashability onto the automotive consumer. One of the fortunate by-products of Naderism is the massive research effort into accident causes, led by the National Highway Traffic Safety Administration and contributed to by many agencies, public and private.

For years we of the automobile buying public had accepted what the large insurance companies told us, but research spurred by serious government concern is proving that many, if not most, of their statements on the subject of traffic safety were only wild guesses.

Remember the safety slogan, "If you drink, don't drive"? The insurance companies were onto something there. If they had started working on the problem of alcoholism years ago, instead of pursuing the insipid policy of propagandizing against drinking drivers, we might have eliminated as many as 25,000 traffic fatalities a year. It is a fact, supported by the NHTSA's newest look at the statistics, that more than half of the traffic deaths each year *involve* persons who have consumed enough booze to be legally intoxicated. It must be pointed out that the involvement includes intoxicated pedestrians as well as drivers. Dr. William E. Tarrants of the National Highway Safety Bureau reported that one-half of all accidents causing death to vehicle occupants, one-third of fatal pedestrian accidents, and one-fifth of all injury accidents "are caused at least in part from the use of alcoholic beverages."

Further examination of the problem indicates that Dr. Tarrants is not talking about people who have taken a couple of beers, the so-called social drinkers we have been led to believe are the culprits. He is talking about drivers who were dead drunk when they got behind the wheel. The definition of drunkenness in most states ranges from the consumption of seven to ten ounces of hard liquor by a 160-pound man within an hour of the incident and usually without anything to eat. That's real elbow bending.

The problem isn't simply that a drunk cannot operate a motor vehicle efficiently. Dr. Tarrants points out four additional behavior factors that the drunk driver presents which have not yet been fully explored by science: (1) cultural patterns in recreation, business, courtship, and entertainment; (2) public attitudes; (3) the economic and social forces that favor drinking; and (4) the emotional needs of the drinker that turn him to the bottle. As far as research has been able to determine, the so-called social drinker is not a significant contributor to accidents, but that may be due only to the limitations of research.

Another difficult factor to cope with is the social stigma of a drunk driving arrest and all that it implies. First, while it is socially hip to consume too much booze, it is definitely a bummer to get arrested for it and have to go to jail, even for the night. Second, to get arrested for drunk driving drastically affects many persons' ability to earn a living. A fine and probation often are assessed against first offenders, but the next time the potential penalty is a jail sentence and loss of the driver's license. In our society loss of driving privileges often hampers a person's ability to commute from home to the job. Too often, a suspended license forces the penalized driver to ignore the law and drive without a license, out of economic necessity.

In 1965 the California Department of Motor Vehicles reported that 33 percent of drivers with suspended licenses and 68 percent of those with revoked licenses were found to have driven that year. How did the DMV find out? By examining traffic citation and accident records. So it is fair to say that of 1326 drivers with suspended and revoked licenses that year it is conceivable that every one of them, or at least a large proportion of them, drove illegally. Only a portion were actually discovered and then only because of arrests or accidents. In Michigan's spot check vehicle inspection program, one six-month period turned up more than 2500 drivers on the road who had suspended or revoked licenses or no license at all. In Montana, which has only 392,308 licensed drivers, the highway patrol arrested 5886 drivers without licenses during 1968.

So, rather than clearing the highway of alcoholics, nailing drunk drivers apparently only turns dangerous motorists into lawless, dangerous ones. Traffic officers aren't dumb, and neither are judges. They are aware of reality. It isn't a weakness on the part of a policeman to exercise leniency by writing a lesser citation for a driver who might be suspected of being under the influence of alcohol. If someone else can drive him home, or if he stops to sober up at a coffee shop somewhere, this is often a more practical course of action than a bust. If that were not true, could there be any traffic at all on the streets on New Year's Eve? Some judges even allow their bias toward law-abiding citizens to color their judgment when passing sentence on a convicted drunk driver. If the offender is a wealthy professional man, for example, the judge might relate to him (judges drink, too) and say to himself, "There, but for the grace of God, go I." If the man is a lower-middle-class wage earner, the judge could easily sympathize with the economic hardship a license revocation or jail term might impose on the man's family. Somewhere in the back of the judge's mind there has to be a thought of what a drunk-driving conviction could mean to the offender's future employment, his chances of success in the business world, or his status on his present job if he has to go to jail.

This isn't idle conjecture. In 1964, Pennsylvania state police made 224,193 arrests for traffic violations, but only 587 of them were for drunk driving. At the time, says Ronald M. Weiers in his book *Licensed to Kill,* there were 5.7 million licensed drivers and 3.8 million passenger automobiles registered in the state, not to mention 17,000 saloons. Weiers further commented that if each of the 2500 state troopers had arrested one drunk driver a year the enforcement rate would have risen 400 percent.

Our safety experts, led by the people in the insurance companies, have insisted for years that the key to control of drunk driving was enforcement. Dr. Tarrants reports on a study of 150 motorists arrested for drunk driving compared with 150 "average" drivers selected on the basis of the number of prior arrests. The drunk driving group had 971 arrests compared with 65 for the "normal" group.

In the case of those 150 drunk drivers, enforcement hadn't managed to improve their behavior on the highway. Whom does enforcement affect? If fear of receiving a traffic citation had any effect at all on the driving population, then only a small percentage of drivers—that element in any society which has no respect for the law—would exceed speed limits. The truth is that enforcement or nonenforcement seems to have little effect on the accident rate. The more research that is done into traffic accidents, the more convincing is the argument that the type of traffic enforcement we are all familiar with has little to do with highway safety. Present enforcement consists largely of ticketing speeders, and it serves mainly to provide revenue for local jurisdictions. Traffic officers with sophisticated timing devices, including radar, lie in wait for unsuspecting motorists and pick them off like ducks in a shooting gallery. Only in a small percentage of cases are traffic enforcement officers, employed as trappers, able to apprehend dangerous drivers, and then usually by chance. This cynical employment of traffic-enforcement manpower has the expected effect on careful, experienced motorists. Most of them continue to drive at rates of speed they feel comfortable with, regardless of posted limits, except when they are aware of the presence of police. Then they slow down until the traffic-enforcement "menace" is out of range.

Experienced drivers are not dumb, either. They know instinctively that traffic accidents occur at all speeds, not merely speeds over the posted limits. So they drive the way they feel most at ease, subconsciously setting their own safety values.

Referring again to drunk driving control, there is another complexity—the questioned reliability of the so-called "balloon test" for detecting alcohol levels present in the suspected offender's system. The balloon is the most common field-testing device in use today.

The Insurance Institute of Highway Safety ran tests on commonly used balloons and found that 36 percent of the time the balloons passed drinkers who had a .10 concentration of alcohol in the blood, and 38 percent of the time they flunked persons who had alcoholic levels below this legal limit.

Even if the balloon tests are reliable, there is other statistical evidence to suggest that younger drivers don't need to consume as much alcohol to become hazardous on the highway as veteran drinkers do. And there is the comment by NHTSA's Douglas Toms himself, who claims that the problem of dealing with the drunk driver is how to isolate him. The true drunk, Toms said, goes through life drunk. It is impossible to tell by comparative observation just how drunk he is, because you rarely, if ever, see him sober enough to arrive at a standard by which his drunken behavior can be compared.

Furthermore, excessive drinking has a double deadly effect on driver performance, according to Fred Benjamin of Toms' staff. Not only does it impair performance, "but alcohol gives one the feeling of euphoria, of well being, and makes the driver think he can drive better than ever he could when sober."

The only factor linking drunk driving to the traffic accident dilemma that means anything at this time is statistical. Safety people now claim that if they could remove all the drunks from the road we would see an immediate 50 percent decrease in traffic fatalities. We can't do that, and until we can the only solution to the drunk-driving problem remains a partial one and a personal one for all of us: to stay out of trouble, one must decline to operate a motor vehicle while drinking, avoid riding with drunks, and be very defensive while driving on the public highways near anyone who is obviously inebriated.

Another area of concern to the accident researchers is the involvement of young drivers. Insurance companies penalize youth by assigning enormously high rates to young drivers. They base this practice on statistical tables that point the finger of blame at young drivers.

The insurance rate for a seventeen-year-old driver is 2.54 times the normal rate. By the time the insured driver reaches age twenty-four he pays a premium of only 1.54 for his insurance. As he grows older, or gets married, the driver is rewarded with a reduction in insurance premiums. In the case of the young student, some companies offer premium discounts for maintaining good grades, on the basis that good marks in school are related to a responsible attitude toward society and less free time to goof around in an automobile. The married driver has fewer accidents than the single or divorced driver, and he is rewarded with lower rates. Women have fewer accidents than men, and they pay lower insurance rates than men the same age. Until fresh research was begun by the government, nearly all the opinions safety officials had about driver performance were influenced by what the insurance tables revealed.

Americans have a great fascination with statistics. Figures don't lie, all that sort of thing. The fact is that figures do tell the truth, but trouble begins when analysts, well intentioned as they may be, try to interpret the figures, to tell us what they really mean.

Consequently, the fact that young drivers are involved

in an excessively high percentage of accidents and far more than their share of injury and fatal accidents has led to many well meaning, but so far unsuccessful, programs to improve the young driver's performance. The fact that males are involved in traffic accidents more often than females, and single men more than married men, has tended to form an image in the minds of traffic-enforcement officials and safety experts, an image of the irresponsible young, male driver—often referred to as a hot-rodder—who combines ignorance of the operation of his car with bravado and a lack of consideration for the rights of other motorists. Another fact emerges from the insurance industry's statistical tables to reinforce this image: that drivers of foreign sports cars and American so-called "muscle cars," both of the type more likely to be driven by younger people, are involved in more than their statistical share of accidents than the more conservative types of vehicles.

Still another factor influences this image, the enforcement picture. Drivers of sporty cars are subject to more citations than drivers of four-door plain-Jane sedans. Any driver of an MG, Alfa, Triumph, AMX, or Shelby GT knows the unfortunate truth of that statistical sidelight. It's based on the same principle as cutting the calf with the white spot on his back out of the herd of 100 head of cattle. The eye of the law focuses just as naturally as anyone else's eye on the smart, sharp machine as it goes by the the blur of traffic. But insurance analysts grind out a different, more sinister implication: that anyone who is attracted enough to own a "flashy" type of transportation, a Corvette rather than a Malibu, a hemi-Charger instead of a Monaco, a Porsche in place of an Audi, is inherently an unsafe motorist. In the ordered world of the insurance company, there is a young punk out there on the road who is a menace. However, as the years go by, this stripling mellows and matures and somehow gains in wisdom and restraint. By the time he has reached the age of twenty-five his wild oats have been sowed, thank Heaven, and he is at last safe enough to be accorded the same respect for his driving ability, the same insurance rates as other, older and more experienced drivers have enjoyed for years.

Anybody who has had to pay insurance premiums based on this absurdity knows that the typical young driver is not irresponsible. The typically irresponsible street-racing goon, the bully behind the wheel, the absent-minded, unthinking clod, the psychologically unfit, the candidate for Skid Row—none of these types ever change appreciably. They either get killed or continue to drive erratically and dangerously the rest of their days. What common sense tells the average driver, the government is now proving with new statistics which hopefully will put an end to the false picture of accident-proneness of young drivers.

To begin with, insurance rates based on age don't take exposure into account. Exposure is a measurement that expresses how frequently one drives under conditions which are statistically "accident conditions."

Generally speaking, more serious accidents occur between the hours of one and four A.M. than at other times of the day, and more accidents happen on weekends than during the week. Those are times when a higher percentage of younger motorists are likely to be driving; therefore, they have greater exposure than older drivers to the periods of highest accident involvement. That doesn't necessarily make young drivers more unsafe, only more exposed.

Ezio C. Cerrelli of the Mathematical Analysis Division of NHTSA has developed a new method of computing the crash-riskiness of various classes of drivers. By his method of analysis it is possible to argue that there are few if any statistical conclusions one can make about drivers according to their age or sex. In fact, a male driver under twenty years of age is statistically less hazardous than a male over sixty-four and only slightly more hazardous than a young woman of his age or a female over sixty-four.

Cerrelli developed a method of rating called the Hazard Index, which takes into consideration the amount of exposure a given driver has and the number of times the same driver is at fault in accidents. By comparing the Hazard Index with the other two factors, exposure and fault, it is easy to see how statistics linking younger drivers with high accident rates can be misleading.

Examining the exposure index, it can be seen that, generally speaking, as a person ages he or she is less likely to

Age Groups	Relative Exposure Index Male-Female	Liability Index Male-Female	Hazard Index Male-Female
Under 20	2.08-1.16	2.44-1.32	1.18-1.14
20-24	1.76-0.93	1.74-0.90	0.99-0.96
25-34	1.34-0.74	1.20-0.66	0.89-0.89
35-44	1.02-0.69	0.92-0.62	0.90-0.90
45-54	0.99-0.58	0.93-0.56	0.95-0.97
55-64	0.84-0.49	0.87-0.54	1.04-1.10
Over 64	0.68-0.42	0.94-0.63	1.39-1.51
All groups	1.21-0.72	1.21-0.71	1.00-0.99

be exposed to ideal conditions for an accident. The liability index shows a high rate for under-twenty drivers, decreasing through the relatixely productive years of life until retirement age, when it takes a jump upward. The curve is much flatter in the hazard index, showing the optimum safety ages for both sexes between twenty-five and forty-four, an age group which takes in most of the driving population. This study shows that the relation of exposure to accident involvement is far more significant than age or sex.

An obvious cause of accident involvement in younger drivers is their lack of experience. Common sense dictates the theory that accidents are more likely to happen to inexperienced drivers. Fred Benjamin of the NHTSA, a senior research psychologist, speaks more to the point:

"Inexperienced drivers who may be teenagers, but the same applies to adults, generally have quite a lot of experience as passengers in cars. They know what can be done in cars. They have the feeling, now I'm behind the wheel, now I can do the same thing. But actually they don't have the experience yet. This relationship of risk to actual lack of experience is responsible for the marked increase of accidents in the first two years of driving."

There is another fallacy about accident involvement that is perpetuated by the insurance companies. It's the belief that a small number of people cause a large percentage of all the accidents. On that assumption the insurance companies penalize those who have had an accident or who have been convicted of traffic violations with higher rates. A motorist who has had an unusual number of accidents will have to carry "assigned risk" automobile insurance. Assigned risk insurance carries a penalty rate on the basis of the driver's statistical liability to have another accident.

A study by Dr. B. J. Campbell of the Highway Research Center at Chapel Hill, North Carolina, reveals that there is almost no link between the number of violations and accidents a person has had and the likelihood that he or she will have an accident in the future.

Most accidents, Dr. Campbell said, involved drivers who had no records of traffic violations for the previous two years. Those with violations were involved in more accidents than persons with no record at all, but the number was so small as to be insignificant. He concluded:

"If you took all drivers with three or more violations in the past two years off the highway and kept them off 100 percent effectively for two whole years, North Carolina would still experience 96.2 percent of the accidents it would have had anyway. Moreover, of the drivers removed from the highway, 71 percent of them would not have been involved in an accident anyway."

Modern safety analysis, conducted by scientists using computers, is performing a very useful function by trying to assign at least some of the blame for accidents and to seek ways to modify some of the terrible consequences of accidents. NHTSA researchers are reporting back that so many variables are linked with the causes of most accidents, that attempts to remedy causes one at a time are not producing results. Except in one area. We are all familiar with the effort to discover who is causing the accidents and why, but there is another important effort in progress to work out injury reduction techniques. This is the much maligned campaign to produce a "car that is safe to crash in." Injury reduction actually goes much further. It involves removing safety hazards from the road and re-engineering unsafe highways. Work in injury reduction had been greatly neglected until recently, but it is rapidly advancing in the face of political roadblocks and despite some controversial detours into questionable techniques such as the passive passenger restraints. The most common of these, and the most criticized, is the "air bag" which inflates upon impact to reduce injury to people inside a crashing car.

Due to the tremendous financial demands to carry out such a program, however, very little is being done to teach defensive maneuvers for avoiding accidents or lessening their effects. "Always drive defensively," say the sloganeers, but what does that mean when you are locked into fast-moving traffic on the freeway and, suddenly, somebody traveling toward you crosses the divider into your path? What do you do as a defensive driver? Denise McCluggage, the woman race driver turned safety lecturer, claims that some drivers who were assumed to have "lost control of their cars" in an emergency didn't actually lose control. They abdicated it. There really is something you can do when you are plunged into an impossible situation. She advises that you extend the area of your accident and stretch the time during which it takes place, and claims this expansion of space and time are guaranteed to lessen the severity of your accident. She lists seven rules to observe:

1. Always dodge trouble to the right—away from oncoming traffic.

2. Always drive off the road rather than skid off.

3. Always hit something soft before you hit something hard.

4. Always hit something going your way before you hit something stationary.

5. Always hit something stationary a glancing blow.

6. Always hit something stationary before you hit something coming toward you.

7. Never hit anything head-on.

All right, what are you going to do about that head-on? If there is time, honk. The oncoming driver may be dozing off or disoriented, and the noise might be enough to awaken him in time. Find an escape route, preferably to the right, because if you try to go to the left and the other driver corrects his direction, you are his one and only target. If you are hemmed in by traffic and there is no hole to the right, make one, even if it means leaning on another car: Denise's Rule No. 4. If you have to drive completely off the road to get out of the way, drive off the road. A car is not limited to a roadway in a situation like this. Drive around anything that is stationary: a tree, a power pole, a parked car, a house; just keep driving and don't lock up the wheels and lose control. If your only choice is a tree or that head-on, it's a poor choice, but take the tree. If there is no way to miss that head-on, crank the steering wheel as hard as you can and spin. If luck is with you, Mister Head-On may go by you as if your car were some sort of revolving door. Or he may strike a glancing blow. The worst that could happen, a T-bone blow amidships at the driver's or passenger's door, is little worse than the head-on crash you would have had by doing nothing. They are both disastrous. In any event, do not abdicate control of your car. Know what course of action improves your chances of survival, and take it.

There is another obvious precaution a smart driver always takes against the statistical probability that he may be involved in an accident. He will have engaged his seat belt and shoulder harness. W. D. Nelson, a General Motors safety engineer, studied 230 accidents in which vehicle occupants wore the proper restraining devices. These were horrendous impacts, some so violent the victims had to be cut out of their cars, but only two persons lost their lives. One of the fatalities might have been caused by a faulty safety harness, and the other conceivably might have been prevented if the victim had adjusted his harness properly, although the chances were very slim. These are some of the 230 accidents cited by Dr. Nelson which did not result in death:

(1) At 60 miles an hour the left rear tire blew out. The untrained driver left the roadway and rolled over two or three times. The roof caved in almost to the level of the hood (sixteen inches of deformation on the right side), but the driver, a twenty-nine-year-old woman, was hospitalized with cuts and bruises—some from the shoulder harness—and a sore back.

(2) A 245-pound male driver left the road on a curve,

struck a large mail box, a twenty-inch-diameter tree, then sideswiped three more trees the same size before the automobile stopped. These repeated hits typically multiply injuries when the vehicle's occupants bounce around inside the vehicle. There is also a high probability of ejection, which quite often is fatal. But the belts held the driver firmly, and his injuries consisted of bruises around the nose and eyes and a cut on the left hand. The car was totaled.

(3) Traveling about 60 miles an hour, a thirty-eight-year-old driver wearing his seat belt, but with his shoulder harness adjusted loosely was suddenly confronted with an oncoming car which had wandered into his path. He wrenched the wheel to the right and went off the road to get out of the way. At 40 mph he struck a tree six inches in diameter. The force was so great that the grille of the car was pushed back more than three feet. Although collisions this severe are almost fatal, the driver emerged with a one-inch cut over his right eye, a sore shoulder, and assorted bruises. He didn't even require hospitalization.

On the other hand, the following are examples of accidents from NHTSA reports in which restraining devices were not used:

(1) Five teenage boys stole a convertible and drove down a divided highway toward a curve. The driver panicked and hit the brakes when he apparently thought he wasn't going to make it. The car impacted the guard rail and ejected the driver, who was decapitated by the guard

rail. The car continued 289 feet down the road, where it banged into the rail again and slid along it scrubbing off sheet metal. The front-seat passenger hit the windshield and dashboard, suffering head injuries. Two of the three back-seat passengers were also injured. The car's owner had installed seat belts even though the car had not come equipped with them originally. The accident analyst supposed that the fatality and some injuries might have been prevented by use of lap belts.

(2) An intoxicated driver, who had many years of driving experience, was not wearing the lap belt installed in his car. A bump in the roadway caused the car to veer out of control and roll over three times, partially ejecting the driver. The car came to rest with the driver's head pinned between the car and the pavement. He was dead on arrival at the nearby hospital.

(3) An expensive foreign sports car left the divided highway in a construction zone, roaring onto a torn-up median separator strip at 80 miles an hour. Both the driver and his passenger were drunk by legal definition (the driver had .13 concentration of alcohol in his blood, his passenger .16). The car rolled over and bounced several times through the torn-up median strip. Both occupants were ejected and died of head injuries.

The occupant restraint system and its ability to modify the injuries sustained in an accident is unchallenged, yet only 10 percent of those motorists who have them in their cars use them. This refusal of drivers and passengers to make use of potentially life-saving equipment has resulted in the government and private agencies launching into their crusade for passive restraints, the kind the motorist doesn't have to activate and has no choice about using. Regardless of the merits of the air bag, and whether or not all cars will eventually come equipped with them, intelligent motorists intent on escaping death or serious injury in an accident situation should make use of harnesses already available in their automobiles.

Of course, the best strategy for avoiding accidents or reducing injuries is to try to drive your way out of trouble. But it is difficult to practice evasive driving effectively unless you understand the principles of car control. Denise McCluggage explains them very neatly:

1. **Brakes don't stop your car, they stop the wheels. Tires stop the car.**
2. **The steering wheel doesn't turn your car, it aims your front wheels. The rolling tires turn the car.**
3. **Brakes can stop your wheels from turning without stopping your car.**
4. **Brakes thus locked can cancel your steering.**

As practiced during the accident-avoidance portion of Bob Bondurant's driving course, the handling of a motor vehicle under panic conditions was not only informative but fun. Bondurant's instructors showed our class an insurance-company movie on skid control and took us out to the school's own skid pad and proceeded to demonstrate how wrong the safety film was.

To Bondurant's knowledge, this is the only film ever

produced on skid control. The fact that it gives misleading instructions is typical of the whole safety issue. So little attention has been paid to real driver performance that even the people who are supposed to know what they are doing aren't always right.

The school's skid-pad car is equipped with dual braking controls so that the instructor, sitting in the right-hand front seat, can cause either the front or back wheels to lock up under braking. In this way he can show the students what happens and how to cope with either condition.

Front-wheel lockup caused the steering to be useless. No matter how hard the wheel was turned, the car continued going in a straight line. When the brake was released, the front wheels resumed steering the car, and quick maneuvering of the steering wheel became necessary to recover control of the car.

Rear-wheel lockup caused the back end to come around. By holding the steering wheel in a straight-ahead position, the result was a 180-degree loop, and the car continued moving in the direction it had originally been going—but it was facing backward. A foot planted hard into the clutch pedal prevents the car from stalling out and possibly doing damage to the engine or gears.

After a little practice, it was possible to induce "180s" and even "360s," which could be driven through in one continuous motion or by inducing two opposing 180-degree spins—one to the right, the other back to the left.

Skidding is not necessarily a disastrous situation, if you master the art of controlling the skid. With practice on a skid pad, you can learn to pull out of a slide and move over one, two, or three lanes at the same time, whichever option you select.

Under normal braking there is seldom any danger of locking up the front or rear wheels, so the reason you need to practice controlled sliding is to prepare yourself for the day a panic stop throws you out of control on the expressway, and the back end of the car is coming at you with a speed differential of 30 to 40 miles an hour.

Bondurant and many other skilled professional race drivers don't believe in braking their way out of emergencies. They would rather drive their way out. If both courses of action are open to you, hit the gas and go. It's always better to be past a potential accident than heading for it.

That is the principle Bondurant tries to teach with his accident simulator. It consists of a short straightaway leading to a one-lane-wide entrance where the approaching car trips an electric eye device that operates three traffic lights. At the start of the run all three lights are green, meaning the three lanes they control are open and safe. When the car enters the accident simulator two of the signal lights change to red, leaving only one lane open. The driver must make a quick evasive maneuver to get into the correct lane. If he should strike a pylon guarding the approach to that lane, he has involved himself in a theoretical fender-bender. If he misjudges and goes through a lane where the light has turned red, he has been wiped out in a "fatal" accident.

The student begins by approaching the accident simulator at 30 miles an hour. After he masters the technique he raises his speed to 35, 40, and finally to 45. A couple of fellows with exceptional reflexes have managed to take the simulator at 50, but even Bondurant doesn't recommend trying it without a lot of practice at the lower speeds. Once the student has mastered the accident simulator at 45, or thinks he has, the operator of the lights throws him a curve and turns all the lights red to see how the student handles a panic stop.

It's tough, but it's fun to do, and if some of the NHTSA staff who have gone through the school had their way, the accident simulator, the skid pad, and other maneuver training would be incorporated into regular driver-education programs in the schools.

Unfortunately, neither the skid pad nor the accident simulator is available to a driver unless he or she attends a school like Bondurant's. A few communities have set up accident-avoidance courses, and many towns send their emergency-vehicle drivers to special schools. But for most of the nation's drivers there isn't even a place to practice emergency maneuvers.

At least not on the street, there isn't. In the west there are off-road vehicle parks and places set aside for driving dune buggies and four-wheel-drive vehicles off the pavement. In the dirt, conditions are similar to what they are on wet pavement, very slippery. There is nothing that builds your confidence for that moment of terror in traffic better than "hanging it out" in the dirt, getting the feel of breaking the back end of the car loose and directing the car to go where you want it to go despite the lack of traction.

In the northern and eastern states there is a form of competition that is also great for skid training—ice racing. Driving in competition on a slippery surface is more than a fun sport—it's excellent schooling for survival in a motor vehicle under one of its most difficult operating conditions and in one of its most hostile environments.

Ken Dunipace of the NHTSA observed that every year when the first snows of winter mush up the street in the Midwest a rash of accidents is certain to result. Many of the drivers involved have twenty to thirty years of experience driving on icy roads in winter. But it's the first exposure of the year that catches them off guard. They crash into something before they have time to adjust to icy driving conditions. In a day or two their technique comes back with practice, and the accident rate goes back to normal for the rest of the winter, Dunipace said. He speculates that this means a short ice-driving refresher course is all that most drivers need to adjust themselves to the hazardous road conditions.

One important element of an accident is that the victim is caught off guard. He's not expecting it to happen. Therefore, one of the solutions to the problem is to anticipate the accident, expect it to happen. Policemen usually don't practice using their pistols at the firing range for recreation. They want to be confident of their ability to use a gun when they have to. Firemen drill all the time, even though most of the calls they answer are routine and many are false alarms. A good driver practices emergency driving, and this practice, rather than the authorities' feeble attempts at speed-law enforcement and their pathetic driver-education programs, is meaningful to highway safety. A good high-performance driver doesn't show up in the statistics by which safety is judged, but he is a more important influence than all of the schools, traffic tickets, and safe-driving slogans in the world.

The high-performance driver is, first, alert; he makes every effort to stay out of trouble by employing the tactics we have already discussed. Second, as he drives along he practices for his accident by playing a little mental game. It's called "What if . . . ?"

The car in front is proceeding smoothly down the street at 40 miles an hour. "What if . . ." the driver, suddenly, without warning, turns left, or slams on the brakes, or blows a tire? You make a mental note of what you would do in any of these events.

"What if . . ." the truck coming up on the right, slowing for the yield sign, doesn't yield? "What if . . ." the pedestrian talking to a friend at the next corner steps off the curb into the crossing zone without looking? And if he does and you are committed to a panic stop, "what if . . ." the car behind or on your right doesn't stop? "What if . . ." you start with the green light at the intersection and suddenly there is a car bearing down on you at 40 mph, obviously going through the red signal? Where do you go, and how?

None of these situations has really happened, but you have imagined the worst and have trained yourself to make a decision under duress. One day the worst may happen, and you'll be ready when it does—ready to act instead of becoming a statistic.

5

Advanced Driving Techniques

The trucking industry has influenced the public with a very subtle public-relations campaign. Nearly everybody believes that truck drivers are better drivers than anybody else on the road.

They should be. They're professionals. They drive not for pleasure but to make a buck. They drive more miles, and they have greater responsibilities. They have special skills to handle their special equipment. A truck driver who crashes too often will have to go out and find other work, if he is still alive to seek it.

To get a license a truck driver must undergo a far more severe licensing procedure. Both the written and driving examinations are tougher by several degrees than those you or I can expect when we go down to the motor vehicle department and apply for a license to drive an automobile. Even the traffic laws are different for truckers. They have different speed limits, they are confined to certain streets and certain lanes, they need special permits and licenses, they have to weigh in at designated stations, and they are expected to observe lower-gear warnings on the grades—warnings that other motorists usually don't even notice. Trucks are tougher to manage. They are heavier, sometimes top-heavy, and they are wind resistant. Tractor-trailer rigs are hinged so they may jackknife and are very difficult to stop in an emergency when fully loaded. Truckers must know the techniques of weight balance if they want their rigs to handle properly in any kind of conditions, but especially in snow, ice, rain, or wind. They must know how to prevent load shifting. They must plan their trips intelligently, because when they are in populated areas, or often when nearing their destinations, they have to route themselves around restricted streets. Long-haul truckers have the additional pressure of keeping to time schedules in the face of bad weather, changing traffic conditions, and the ever-present danger of speed traps from one end of the country to another.

Most of all, truck drivers have to maintain super alertness for hours on end to avoid the ridiculous pitfalls that motorists create for them. Truckers have the same trouble you or I have staying away from the idiots, but they do not have nearly the maneuverability in a 50,000-pound rig or even much smaller haulers.

The truth is not, however, that truck drivers are somehow superior human beings at the wheel of a motor vehicle. The talent of the good truck driver is derived from his experience. Experienced truckers are, by and large, good drivers, but a representative share of the nation's truck drivers are just plain terrible at the wheel. Some are dangerous because of their lack of experience, others for psychological reasons, and still others because of their inability to cope with mechanical things.

Why would a trucker suffer from lack of experience?

After all, he has chosen driving as a profession. The sad truth is that chauffeuring (driving for a living) is one of the lowly forms of employment in our society. Youngsters growing up might crave a career as a policeman or a fireman, but very few children dream of the day when they can drive their own trucks. By the time a young man or woman reaches the age of decision regarding his or her life's work, the glamour jobs are in the professions or commerce or in show business or athletics or government or journalism, not truck driving. Most young people who prefer to work with their hands, as opposed to sitting at a desk in an office, go into the trades. A lot of them do not consider trucking as a skillful line of employment. Consequently, the truck-driving recruit often suffers from lack of motivation as well as lack of experience. He's in it for the money or because something else he would prefer to do isn't available to him.

Every trade, indeed even professions such as medicine and the law, can count on a certain number of people who are trained to do the work only to drop out. Trucking is a good example. As a business, it is highly competitive and subject to wide fluctuations in profit according to the demand for services, and this in turn causes ups and downs in the demand for drivers. Every time the demand is low, many skillful truckers leave the field, never to return, and when demand is high new drivers come along who need training and experience at the wheel. I wouldn't even begin to guess the percentage of these beginners on the highways, but I suspect it has been quite high in recent years, from my own experiences and observations over a long period of time.

The psychological factors, which we have already touched on, are more glaring when they apply to truckers, because truck drivers wield a lot more clout when they crawl up on your rear bumper than someone in a sedan. If it's power they crave to assert when they take out their aggressions on the traffic, truck drivers find themselves well armed to assert it.

If a trucker can't deal with mechanics, it implies that he is misplaced in his occupation and ought to get into some other line of work. There are a few such truck drivers; in the absence of statistics we imagine their numbers are very small.

Truly, the record of the trucking industry, measured by accidents per mile and per ton-mile traveled, is much better than the record of the general driving public. A more serious and growing problem, one that hits closer to home as far as you and I are concerned, is the threat to highway safety of make-believe truck drivers—poorly licensed and ignorant operators of recreational vehicles.

They're everywhere. Owners of campers are the worst offenders. Their vehicles are top-heavy, under-tired, aerodynamically poor, and driven as if there were no tomorrow. They are often used the same way trucks are, to stow a lot of cargo, and much of the time their cargo shifts dangerously, causing the camper to list one way or the other, or to sway in the wind just short of spinning out of control. On multi-laned highways and freeways they frequently control the fast lane, while trucks are restricted to the right-hand lanes. If RVs (recreational vehicles) are traveling at the same rate as the freeway traffic flow, their drivers are often driving beyond their own capabilities or dangerously near the limit of the capabilities of the vehicle.

Frequently, campers are towing something. Sometimes it is a trailer with camping gear. It may be a boat, a rig to carry bikes or motorcycles, or a dune buggy hitched to the rear bumper. Among the absurdities I have observed is a camper towing both a trailer and a boat, one behind the other. It's strictly illegal, but some people, in their ignorance, will do it.

Private citizens who tow a trailer are frequently a menace on the road because of their lack of experience. The typical trailer is a U-haul, and the motorist is probably moving from one apartment to another, saving the price of a moving bill. You can't blame him. The law states only that he must obey all traffic laws and be licensed to drive an automobile. If he packs the trailer correctly and doesn't go over the speed limit, he won't get in any trouble with the law, but if a panic situation presents itself, he's in for plenty of trouble of a different kind.

Another towing driver is the fellow who is taking his boat to a lake or his vacation trailer to a campsite. He is often more experienced, but there is nothing he has to do in the way of education or licensing that would adequately equip him to haul anything. He may not even be aware that the handling of his sedan has been drastically changed by adding on the trailer.

The vacation trailer and the camper have led to another recreation development: the vacation home on wheels, otherwise known as the motor home. Most of them are veritable yachts of the highways. They're too cramped to live in for more than short periods of time, but they are large enough to be comfortable on the road as well as at the campsite. They contain kitchens, refrigerators, bathrooms, bedrooms, dining nooks. They are usually air conditioned, and often they are equipped with stereo entertainment.

Their handling requires an operator's license, nothing more. But motor homes are not for the ordinary driver who has merely passed the simple automobile license examination. These vehicles perhaps are not under-tired, because the manufacturers are responsible enough in most cases to shoe them properly, but they have a higher center of gravity than an automobile and require a different level of driving skill. They are like barn doors in the wind, and therefore are not capable of accelerating as well as a car. Their enormous mass is hard on brakes. Because there is space enough inside the typical motor home for several people to walk around at the same time, the load is capable of shifting. The size of the mass makes it susceptible to wild gyrations if the driver strikes a pothole or a bad bump.

Motor homes range in price from that of converted vans costing less than $5,000 to super elegant $100,000 palaces; but since most are in the $10,000 to $20,000 class, they are within the range of most middle class families. They take the place of a vacation cottage or a boat and can be used for basic transportation in an emergency.

A motor home drives somewhat like a bus, with such luxuries, usually, as automatic transmission, air conditioning, and power assists. Most manufacturers claim that anybody who can drive a car can drive a motor home, but we regard that claim as misleading. There may be no special license required, but the handling is a lot different. It is true that a motor home can be driven by just about anybody, but it takes practice and the exercise of extraordinary good sense to get the most out of one. At three tons and up, they don't handle like Corvettes. It's not recommended that you attempt to break the Land Speed Record for motor homes held by Alex Tremulis, who sped two ways across El Mirage Dry Lake in California at an average speed of 97.613 mph in a Travoy on May 16, 1970. The manufacturer sponsored his run, but doesn't recommend that customers try to go that fast in anybody's motor home. I agree.

Campers, cars with trailers attached, and motor homes are special vehicles and require special driving techniques. It's not enough to know that their purpose is to get away from traffic, to go to remote places where the hazards of other vehicles are no longer present. To get there it is necessary to drive on the highway where the traffic is, just as truck and bus drivers do. When you leave the highway for the lonely country road, there is a new set of conditions —poor pavement, rural traffic popping up unexpectedly, winding mountain roads, poor sign marking. Eventually, there is a third condition, off-the-road driving that most professional truck drivers seldom encounter. Gerry Gross, marketing vice-president of Sportscoach of America, Inc., estimates that at least 80 percent of all motor homes are driven off-the-road. That's not a guess. It is based on his company's research. Driving off the road is, by and large, the reason most people buy recreation vehicles. They want to go places that are away from where other people are. They want to go where the fish are biting or where they can collect rocks or ride their motorcycles or sleep under starry skies. Those places are usually miles off the pavement.

Neither the federal nor state governments require special licensing for driving recreational vehicles or for special driving situations such as towing or heavily loaded cars. If you want to do this type of driving, it is best to be trained, or at least prepared for it, on your own.

Campers, vans, and motor homes handle quite a bit like trucks. Sometimes they have standard transmissions, and a few of them have compound gearing or four-wheel drive. If you are not familiar with declutching and shifting gears, practice before you drive any long distance. In larger vehicles, subject to the gearing-down regulations which trucks must observe on the highway, it is a necessity to learn double clutching. We already discussed it in Chapter Two, but it would be wise to go over the procedure again.

The shifting knob in a truck, as in a race car, is usually to the right of the steering wheel, and the shift lever extends out from the floor. Few gearshifts are located on the steering column anymore, but if they are you can adjust to them easily. The correct position for the right hand is to cup the knob, fingers over the front and the heel of the palm over the back of the knob. The gearshift should be pushed forward with the heel of the palm or pulled backward with the fingers. The shift pattern of most four-speed boxes is in the shape of the letter "H," with first gear top left, second bottom left, third top right, fourth bottom right, and neutral in the crossbar. Reverse can be off to either side, top or bottom. In trucks with compound gears this varies. A few minutes familiarizing yourself both with the gear lever travel and its feel when being shifted are well spent.

A simple, smooth shifting motion requires pushing in the clutch pedal and smoothly pushing the gearshift forward into first, releasing the clutch pedal smoothly while gradually pressing the throttle. From first to second is a simple pull back, second to third a push up and to the right, third to fourth straight back.

Double clutching adds one operation during the shift, at the time the lever has shifted the gears into neutral. At that point the clutch pedal is freed to match engine speed to road speed, which smooths the transition from one gear to another; then the clutch pedal is pushed in again while completing the gear change. Matching the engine speed to the road speed when downshifting requires a quick blip of the throttle to speed up the engine.

Double clutching is a necessity in downshifting large vehicles, and it helps smooth out the upshift as well. It can be a little tricky to learn at first, but once mastered is a very smooth, easy maneuver. Most RVs of the light truck, van, and bus variety should be double clutched to help transmissions last and to smooth out their acceleration and deceleration.

Turning with campers, vans, and motor homes is different from automobiles because of their higher center of gravity. While the wheels take the bottom part of the vehicle, the part to which they are attached, in the direction of the turn, the top part of the RV wants to go in the direction it was traveling, and the vehicle leans over, away from the direction of the turn. In other words, when you turn right, the vehicle wants to fall over on its left side.

Once the vehicle has turned the corner and the springing action of the suspension has done its work, the top of the RV swings back to the right and wants to lean the vehicle over on that side. If the vehicle doesn't turn over to either left or right side by then, quite often it becomes afflicted with what motorcyclists recognize as high-speed wobble. The RV shudders back and forth wildly, increasing its swings until it gets off balance enough to tip over.

There are several cures. The first and most obvious is to beef up the suspension so that the vehicle counteracts tilting with a tendency toward stability. You could go even further by purchasing one of the anti-sway kits available on the market which counterbalance the vehicle's tendency to tip over. A Chevy pickup with a camper body is not a Ferrari Berlinetta. It doesn't corner in the same way. That means slow down for corners and avoid the first sway, the one which leads to that disastrous series of wobbles.

Hard braking creates a similar condition. You are familiar with the diving of race cars when they brake. The rear end becomes light and the nose dips almost to the pavement. In a more exaggerated way, that is what happens to top-heavy RVs under braking. The mass of the vehicle wants to continue, while the wheels under the mass want to stop. The load multiplies on the front wheels and the rear wheels become light.

At these times the RV is on the verge of swerving out of control, much more so than an automobile would be, because the movement of the mass above the center of gravity is fighting against the forces operating below the center of gravity.

Another factor affecting handling is the center of balance. If you become accustomed to driving the pickup truck before the camper body goes on, you will understand. The pickup is a keen machine. Compared with most cars it has great acceleration in the low speed ranges. The heavy duty suspension makes it feel like a sports car in the turns. Heavy duty brakes make it stop on a dime, comparatively. But put a camper body on, and it's a different vehicle. The center of balance has been moved backward, from near the front wheels to near the rear wheels. The extra bulk gives it nearly twice the wind resistance, lowering acceleration. The raised center of gravity makes it wobbly in the corners. The most noticeable of these changes is the rearward move of the center of balance.

The first thing you notice is that you don't look out of the windshield the same any more. The back end has lowered, and you sight the road ahead at a slightly different angle. If you sit very short in the driver's seat and the sun is low and straight ahead, you notice it right away because the sun visor no longer comes down low enough to shade your eyes.

Two basic changes in the center of balance should influence the way you now drive. One is that with more weight added to the rear wheels there is comparatively less on the front; therefore, the steering will feel differently. At higher speeds it will become very noticeable, if not before. The second change is that weight shifting will feel a great deal differently than it did. Under hard acceleration, when weight tends to roll back onto the rear wheels, the steering will feel very light. Under heavy braking, unless it is absolutely straight ahead, the camper will lean more easily to one side or another.

Without knowing these things, most people fight their campers until they get a sort of intuitive feel. They may not understand the reasons why the camper handles the way it does, but they learn to cope with its "eccentricities." With some exceptions, most camper drivers know better than to drive in a high wind, and they learn to adjust to shifting winds and gustiness. They unconsciously look ahead to see if they are about to come out from behind a hill or a sand dune that might be sheltering them from a wind. When turning a corner they slow down.

Unfortunately, many camper owners never do learn how to tie down the groceries, extra motorcycles, and other cargo they carry to resort areas inside their rolling cabins. Under emergency conditions these masses roll around and often change the stability of the camper drastically from one moment to the next.

Whenever there is a choice of where to put something, use the floor, not the bunks. Tie it down or wedge it in such a way that it cannot move. If there is a choice of the front or the rear of the cabin, pack it as near to the front of the vehicle as possible to offset the extra weight in the rear. Never pack one side and not the other. It's easy to remember: Down low, forward, to the center of the aisle, and secured.

You may never notice any effect on handling on the highway, but once you get off the pavement into the dirt, the value of intelligent packing will demonstrate itself.

One of the great adventures in motoring is driving off the road. The term *off the road* is a little misleading, since practically all the driving done off the road is on dirt roads. Some of them are graded, oiled, and graveled or in an equivalent state. Not all dirt roads are bad, and in fact some of them are better than some paved roads. On the other hand, not all dirt roads are as smooth as glass. Particularly in the springtime and after rains, they are pitted, punctuated with washouts, dusty, bumpy, and washboard-like. Some roads are little better than trails, very soft and sandy. Quite often they are dead-ends. There are boulders to smash into, cliffs to drive over, mud holes to bog down in.

Once off the pavement, however, the spirit of pioneering takes over. You know someone has been on the road before you, but you wonder how many times and how recently. A dirt road implies that you are going to an out-of-the-way place, somewhere to get away from it all. It's an exhilarating feeling to drive down a country lane, trees overhanging the road, small animals skittering out of the way, or to roll across the desert on a straight line cut in the sagebrush that ends on the horizon.

It's quite another feeling to get lost, to break down, or to crash. That's when you wish the lonely, deserted road were somehow transformed into the Hollywood Freeway so someone would find you right away. The newspapers every summer report on the tragic situations that people have wandered into, lost in the desert or in the mountains, abandoning their cars and striking off alone across the wilderness to die of heat exposure, dehydration, or a fall from a cliff. Thousands of man hours are spent every year searching for lost hikers and off-road riders in the wilderness.

As a general rule, the poor unfortunates get approximately what they ask for. Getting lost means they weren't prepared adequately for their trip. If they became stuck, either they were not prepared to handle that situation or they didn't use their heads to get free. If they broke down, chances are that they failed to check out the car mechanically before they started the trip, or they lacked some simple mechanical knowledge (such as how to change a tire or temporarily repair a leak in the radiator). If they crashed, the accident was probably no accident—they were simply driving over their heads.

There is no way to tell a motorist how not to get lost. Some people are born with an innate sense of where they are at all times. They are like the legendary household pets who find their way home after being lost on a trip 1500 miles away. Or like the unwanted doggie who was taken out to the desert and abandoned, only to come scratching at the back door three or four days later. It's not enough to know by the sun or the stars which direction is east or west. It's important to know at all times where you are in relation to where you have been as well as where you want to go. In other words, you are never lost until you forget how you arrived at the place where you are.

The safest and simplest guide in the wilderness is a road map of the area, one which lists or even suggests dirt surface back roads. There isn't an area of the United States that doesn't have some sort of mapping, and in the poorest charted place of all, Baja California, there is at least one excellent book available that not only details every trail, but gives historical data on points of interest. Off-road buffs who spend time in off-road heaven—that's Baja—will tell you that Gerhardt & Gulick's *The Lower California Handbook* is a must. If the map you have doesn't give back roads, keep your own mileage readings and judge your direction (a compass would be helpful) in relation to the paved roads it does chart. Road maps like the kind they give away at gas stations are good for pavement travel, but many are deceptive for off-road use. This is particularly true if they don't show section lines, as most good maps do. Section lines are the best gauge of distance traveled when there are no road distances shown on the map, because a section is a square mile, and the lines are one mile apart. If you have a map of the back country area you are exploring, look for the section lines and use them to advantage.

It doesn't help to know where you are if you are stuck. The usual problem is soft ground, not meant to support a vehicle as heavy as the one you are driving. Most of the time four-wheel drive conquers this situation, because it is tough to get all four wheels stuck at the same time. The typical mud or sand trap is one in which you have caught the rear driving wheels. It usually happens because you were traveling too slowly, and the momentum of the car wasn't enough to overcome the lack of traction underfoot. That's something to remember if you are thinking in terms of not getting stuck. Don't slow down in the soft spots. Often getting stuck is accomplished in a panic situation: The road ahead peters out, or looks unsafe, and the driver stops and tries to turn around to go back. If there is ever any question, you can find out how soft the road is by getting out of your vehicle and walking ahead to look at it first. By the time you look at it from the cab of the RV it may be already too soft to go ahead and even a worse place to turn around. The ruts in which you are running might give you a little traction, but the sand or mud outside those ruts probably won't. It's time to put the RV into reverse and carefully back out to where there is some solid ground for turning around.

Okay, you didn't do any of those things, and you're stuck in the sand. What next? Easy, you dig out the loose stuff from under each rear tire and replace it with something solid, preferably so you can back out of the bad spot. What's that? You forgot to bring a shovel? Don't despair. I've used old boards that were lying around, metal plates, tin cans, hub caps, anything that can simulate a shovel, and in a desperate situation both hands. What do you use under the wheels that is solid? Anything. An old board or two, cardboard cartons, even rocks. If there is no debris handy and you have nothing in the vehicle you can sacrifice to the sand gods, pick up as many large rocks as you can and place them under the wheels. The tires will grab rocks better than they will sand.

The trick to driving out of a trap like this is not to be too anxious to get out quickly. Take your time and make sure everything is in place. If the car won't ease out, don't gun the motor and try to blast your way out. That will only succeed in digging you in deeper. Ease out of the hole carefully, and after a few inches of progress, gradually increase your speed so that you won't bog down in another soft spot. The best way to conquer the fear of getting stuck is to get stuck and work your way out of it. It does wonders for your confidence.

There are worse ways to get hung up, but generally they are not the things that will happen to a driver who sticks to dirt roads. Four-wheel-drive vehicles and some dune buggies are equipped to solve these problems, usually with a winch that should be standard equipment if you do much off-the-road traveling. Off-roaders are usually very helpful to those in distress, which means it is a good idea to stick to those areas where other drivers are likely to come by once in a while.

Breaking down for any reason is an inconvenience in the city, but out where the temperature is 120 degrees and there is no shade, or where the thermometer never gets as high as freezing for months at a time, or where there is no help within fifty miles, it is a potential disaster. There is a road race through the highlands of Ecuador for which the drivers make sure their equipment is in top condition, because one of the hazards, should they fall out of the race, is the fierce tribe of poison-dart wielding, cannibalistic savages whom even the government can't control. If a driver breaks down in their territory, he has not only lost the race, he is in danger of losing his ilfe. Caution to prevent breakdowns should be the watchword of all off-roaders, because simple emergencies can easily turn into tragedies. Cannibals lying in wait are not typical perils, but fates just as bad can sometimes result.

The bad things that have happened in the back country seem idiotic in retrospect, but actually they amount to a lack of careful planning and preparation. One fellow with a flat tire stopped and changed it before proceeding. Forty miles later his spare blew out in the midday heat of the Mojave Desert, and there he was, cooking inside his sedan with a wife and two children. He wandered off to get help and was never found. The other three perished in the heat. If he had turned around and gone back to town to repair or replace the flat tire before proceeding, four deaths might have been prevented.

The folks at Bonneville, on the other hand, marveled at a weathered old Australian gentleman who showed up to race his motorcycle at Speed Week one year. He had saved his money for years and sailed to America with his motorcycle for this occasion. With the little money he had left when he arrived he bought an old Studebaker on a Los Angeles used-car lot. He started across the desert in August only to learn he had a leaking radiator. Not deterred, he found an old stick by the side of the road and jammed it into the hole in the radiator. It was a temporary solution, but it worked for a while. The old radiator sprung another leak and another. Each time, he jammed another piece of wood into the hole, like the little Dutch boy's thumb in the dike, and the ancient automobile got him to Bonneville—and back to Los Angeles—before it expired.

The well-prepared off-roader takes with him the temporary helpers that solve problems which may overcome his vehicle when it is away from the ministrations of a trained mechanic. A case of motor oil, digging tools, tire changing and pumping gear, a patching kit, the handful of tools necessary to make minor adjustments or check the engine (wrenches, screwdrivers, friction tape, soft-headed hammer, extra electrical wiring, gauges), an extra set of spark plugs, fan belts, a first-aid kit, matches, extra rations, plenty of water, a crowbar. Does it sound like overkill? The Baja buff would add to that list "a few words of Spanish," because when you're in trouble in the back country of Mexico it may come in very handy. Have you ever seen a mechanic, working with nothing but hand tools, rebuild a front suspension? Or repair a broken transmission case? I have. Mexican mechanics can work absolute wonders.

The best way to train for off-road driving is to become adept at dirt bike riding. Many of the same techniques, problems, and cautions apply to both. Most trouble occurs when the driver or bike rider drives beyond his field of vision. You have to learn to judge distances in the desert and on lonely dirt roads as you proceed, remembering at all times the vital stopping distances that are the limitations of your vehicle and your reaction time. If your reaction time is six-tenths of a second and you are traveling 60 miles an hour, you will cover 53 feet in the time it takes to see the panic situation and take evasive action. That means the tree, rock, or edge of the cliff in your path had better be well beyond the fifty-foot range or you can't miss it. The object of danger should always be beyond the radius of your stopping capability at whatever speed you are traveling, or you will have to choose another means of avoiding it.

While the difference in off-road driving and pavement driving is the surface, the differences in off-road surfaces are even more pronounced. Dirt, sand, rocks, river bottoms, grass, salt—there are countless varieties of ground to drive on, and they all affect traction differently. The softer the surface, the more desirable it is to be moving rapidly. The bumpier the surface, the slipperier it is and the harder to maneuver on it.

Off-road racing vehicles are built with softer suspensions so that they can literally jump barriers and holes. The technique of jumping is similar to the execution of a "wheelie" on a dirt bike. It prevents crashing by keeping the front end up so the hard impacts can be absorbed by the tires, not the nose of the vehicle. Often it is better to accelerate and jump than it is to brake to lessen an impact or dodge an obstacle. Racers who were in the Baja 500 in 1972 swear that Bobby Ferro was jumping so high in his Sandmaster dune buggy that he cleared the tops of trees and leapfrogged over other cars. Most of the other competitors got a good look at him, because he started almost dead last and passed 150 other vehicles on his way to an elapsed-time victory.

Most of Ferro's driving was done at night in that race, because he had such a poor starting position. Everybody marveled at how he overcame that handicap. The running is usually slower at night because the visibility is much poorer. That idea is misleading, however, according to Bob Bondurant, who really prefers night driving in off-road races. Bondurant finds that he gets a better perspective at night. His headlights pick up the depressions, which show as dark shadows, and he can tell how deep and wide the holes are by how dark they are in his headlights.

A lot of what is called off-road driving is actually done on graded dirt roads or on gravel. If you're the kind of driver who really enjoys hanging the rear end of a car out, dirt roads are a gas. As long as there is no traffic and you have the road to yourself, with nothing just off the road to hit should you slide off, you can practice dirt tracking around corners and get the feel of steering with the throttle. It's not wise to drift sideways over rough ground, because that is inviting a flip. But on level ground such as a smooth dirt road, you oversteer in the direction of the turn until the rear end starts to break away just a bit, then turn the wheel slightly back away from the direction of the turn and give it just a bit more throttle. The car will slide sideways, and it will actually turn the corner as you make minute corrections with the steering wheel—even though the front wheels are turned in the opposite direction of the turn. Too much throttle and you spin out. That's why you should never try anything like that if there is the least possibility of hitting anything, until you have the technique mastered absolutely. Good off-roaders can drive right at an obstacle, set their car into a drift and whip it left and right so skillfully that it will miss hitting the target without changing its path.

It's important to remember that the dirt isn't a skid pad. If you rely on it to be slippery and the surface changes, it might suddenly not be slippery any more. Driving in the dirt implies the need for great care in observation and ability to "read" the road ahead.

A driving skill that may not be as exciting to practice, but which is important though seldom taught, is towing. Anybody with the price to rent a U-haul trailer can tow, but hardly anyone spends the money for lessons to learn how to tow properly. Sometimes the rental agency will give advice. Sometimes the dealer who sells the trailer to a boat owner will insist on briefing his customer. Travel trailer manufacturers often provide booklets, and there are many publications on motor homes, vacation trailers, boat trailers, and such "add-ons." However, the first time you try to tow a trailer, you should realize by feel that you have just acquired some new, special-handling problems.

Every state has its own speed limits and special regulations covering trailers of all descriptions. If you're in Rhode Island, don't exceed 35 miles an hour with a trailer. In Nevada you can go as fast as local conditions of safety will permit. Most of the speed limits for trucks apply to cars pulling trailers. All states require proper taillights, brake lights, license plate illumination, and turn signals. These lights are easily made operative by attaching the clip-on wiring, normally provided with the trailer, to the taillight wiring just inside the trunk compartment of the car doing the towing. All states have some safety device requirements, but they are common sense items. The most important of these is a proper hitch. The hitch should be as heavy-duty as the manufacturer recommends and also meet any local safety regulations for both the towing vehicle and the trailer. Outside rear-view mirrors that extend outside the width of any trailer blocking the rear vision of the driver are required in most states and should be mandatory everywhere. Flares, chains, and even fire extinguishers are required in some states. The best policy to follow before hitching up a trailer and going on vacation or renting a U-haul to move to a new apartment is to call the local highway patrol office and ask what the regulations are —safety requirements, necessary licensing, speed limits, and weight restrictions. You will understand why if you're stopped, particularly if you're pulling a U-haul. They are sitting ducks for ticket writers.

Beyond these normal preparations for towing, the most important items are the load you carry and the wheels and tires that are being used to support it.

Trailers run the gamut from small one-wheelers that haul bicycles and motorcycles and camping gear to wide-load cargo carriers that must be pulled by special truck tractors. The towing experience an ordinary motorist is most likely to have will be one of those one-wheelers, a two-wheel U-haul, boat trailer or RV transporter, a vacation trailer, or simply an RV under tow, resting on its own four wheels.

First, is the towing vehicle's suspension up to the job? There are heavy-duty towing packages available, and one of them ought to be used if the load is heavy enough. Second, are the towing vehicle and trailer compatible? Too heavy a load does more than tax the engine and brakes. The rule of thumb is that the trailer and vehicle loaded shouldn't exceed twice the weight of the vehicle empty. Third, does the trailer balance its load well? If it bears down on the hitch, the car's rear end will be depressed, front end lightened, and you will have acquired a bad handling problem before driving away from the curb. Handling may be worse if the trailer hitch lifts up on the rear end.

Since steering is done with the front wheels, you don't have the proper amount of control over the car if the front end is light. If the condition is severe enough, your forward visibility will be restricted, and at night your headlights will not shine where you want them to. They will point too high and may not only be a hazard to oncoming drivers, but may not be effective for you. If the load in the trailer is too far back, it can reduce the traction upon acceleration and braking, and the headlights will be aimed too low.

Now, let's examine the car-trailer combination under dynamic conditions. You already know that when acceleration occurs there is a shifting of weight to the rear wheels, and under braking the weight shifts forward and loads the front wheels. Now, added to this weight movement is the trailer. Just as the weight shifts to the rear of the car under acceleration, so does it shift in the trailer. But the hitch is the "hitch," so to speak. Weight to the rear of the car, rear end goes down. Weight to the rear of the trailer, front end lifts. The hitch equalizes both of these opposing forces.

The car wants to push the hitch down, while the trailer wants to pull it up. If the load is properly balanced and the hitch is secure, you will feel very little of this phenomenon. But if the load is too heavy or unbalanced and the change in speed too abrupt, you are going to have a control problem. If you have a fight with the steering wheel on your hands while trying to accelerate, you will have the same problem or worse when you try to stop.

The handling situation can be even more critical, depending on how well the load is packed in the trailer. On the typical moving day, there are bedsprings, refrigerator, and dining room chairs stacked about the U-haul with little or no thought about weight distribution. But it's something to consider. The best place to carry most of the weight is over the wheels. If you plan the loading so that the freezer, range, or other heavy object is directly over the trailer's axle, you will avoid most weight distribution problems. The center of balance is another weight distribution factor. If the load has two massive objects, place one on the right side and one on the left. If there is only one, center it.

Another handling problem is the effect of your tow vehicle and trailer's new aerodynamics. With the trailer on back, it makes a bigger target for the wind, which means the motor will have to work harder. In crosswinds the trailer can work against you, too, giving the air currents a larger target to buffet. Let's say there is a 40-mph gust of crosswind trying to push you onto the shoulder. Your car, which used to be a 20-foot target, is now 35 feet long with the addition of a boat trailer. You steer to the left to correct for the buffeting, but that only turns the front wheels to the left, and the trailer now wants to push the car's rear wheels to the right. It's trying to jackknife your whole rig. Chances are that a 40-mph gust won't do more than remind you about the trailer you are pulling, but you will be thankful that you made a smooth corrective movement instead of a jerky one, because a poorly executed move could throw you out of control.

The importance of aerodynamics is emphasized by the frequent highway closures and "Sigalerts" to warn camper drivers and trailer haulers of high winds along certain stretches of highway.

Turning with a trailer in tow isn't normally much of a problem, because the one- or two-wheel trailer merely follows you through the corner if its load is properly anchored. A shifting load, however, coupled with a show-off driver who takes the corner like Stirling Moss, are the only necessary ingredients in the recipe for an accident.

Both the car and its trailer are subject separately to the dynamic forces of cornering, even though they are hitched together. Turn right, and the weight shifts to the left. Brake, and the weight comes forward onto the front wheels. In the trailer that means that weight also wants to shift left, but it can lean backward under extreme conditions. Items could fall out onto the street. The trailer could be tipped over, or jackknifing could result under even more extreme conditions.

The tricky part to learn, backing up with a trailer in tow, requires a skill that few drivers seem to be able to master, although it's very simple. The way to think about it is to imagine the car-trailer combination as a snake crawling backward. If the snake wants his tail to go right, he has to push his tummy to the left to get the tail pointed right. So, to make the trailer go right, first crank the steering wheel to the left to get the back end of the trailer pointed right. Next, bring the steering wheel back to just left of its normal position and continue in reverse until the trailer is going in the precise direction you want it to go. Then it is a question of neutrally steering the car so that it follows the lead of the trailer, the same way the snake's tail would steer the rest of him if he were backing up. As the trailer goes right, steer the car right, and trailer and car will line up straight.

Backing up a trailer properly is a simple task, but it takes a lot of practice, just as the simple skill of parallel parking does. They both require good depth perception, coordination, and simple logic.

Trailer and boat manufacturers make one other excellent suggestion: Keep good track of the condition of the trailer wheel bearings. Boat trailers are always being backed up into the water, which can float away protective grease. Make sure the wheel bearings don't pack up.

It may seem overly cautious to speak of today's expressway driving as "advanced," but, in fact, average motoring speeds have been on the rise since the invention of the automobile. Each year, as roads and vehicles improve, speed limits are increased and traffic flows a bit faster. If you think this statement seems to ignore the temporary 55-mph national speed limit that went into effect in 1974, you are correct. Since most drivers seem to be ignoring this reduced speed limit, we shall too. In any event, ordinary driving conditions have long since advanced beyond standard licensing skill requirements. There are many in the driving population today who remember when pushing the Model A up above 45 miles an hour was exciting and made one feel a bit Barney Oldfieldish. When ordinary passenger cars started exceeding a mile a minute, they were really racy. Three generations ago it was widely believed that a person who drove faster than 60 miles an hour underwent physical and mental changes. Land Speed Record attempt drivers turned their heads sideways to avoid the possible ill effects of letting the wind strike their faces and work changes on them. In those days the terms "breathtaking speeds" and "daredevil" were created. Those fears turned out to be unfounded, but there is a solid basis for believing that each new speed increment creates a new and different environment for the driver. As any racing driver will tell you, each 5 mile-an-hour increment of speed requires a new dimension of alertness. Call it concentration, if you will. Therefore, a person who was licensed to drive when the top speeds were around 55 mph has had to teach himself how to keep up with the 70-mph traffic of the 1970s. The process has been gradual, to be sure, but it has not been without its difficulties.

The training that you should have to zip down the freeway at 70 with the other cars is available only at a few schools like Bondurant's, and so the alternative is to teach yourself. Reaction time isn't nearly as important as judgment. Developing good responses to every possible situation in 70-mph traffic requires exercise of your brain. We have already discussed how to do many of these things, how to "play games" mentally as you drive, how to anticipate new situations, how to second-guess other drivers, how to prepare yourself mentally for the catastrophe that is lurking out there to trap you, even how to crash.

The important thing is to practice, practice, practice. The more you concentrate on making a simple task like driving a car more meaningful, the more pride you will take in your ability and the better a driver you will become.

6

Caring for the Family Pet

It hasn't been too many years since gas station operators started advertising "free air" and calling their businesses "service stations." Before sixty-second service became the vogue, motorists used to carry a hand air pump with them, just in case, and rags to wipe off the windshield. Tire patching kits were kept in the trunk compartment. Drivers were more conscious of their cars' demands for attention, and they were often resourceful about getting Betsy running again whenever she broke down.

When you drive in to fill 'er up today, the service station attendant doesn't need to be asked to clean the windshield. His company has trained him to do the little things that motorists once had to do for their own cars. He will usually raise the hood and check the oil, and sometimes the levels of water in the radiator and in the battery. Exceptionally conscientious fellows will eyeball the tires, and if they are good company men anxious to sell products they will check for other signs of wear and neglect: worn fan belts, hoses and battery cables, dim headlights, and dirty oil. If you ask them, they will check transmission, power system and brake fluid levels or replace used-up dash lights and turn-signal indicator solenoids.

Many people who own automobiles costing $3000 and more depend on their corner service station for everything from changing the oil to major overhauls. Modern stations are basically in business to sell simple replacement parts like tires and batteries, car care products like waxes, and additives for fuel and oil. The services they normally are competent to perform, but sometimes are not, include lubrication and simple electrical tune-ups. Some corner stations have automatic car washes. A few have a mechanic on duty to do repair work, or they have an arrangement with an independent garage nearby, sometimes right on the property or next door. Enterprising station owners in the right circumstances operate towing services and rent U-haul trailers. Larger, usually company-owned stations specialize in diagnostic clinics that check the health of your car with electronic probes and measure the efficiency of its engine with wave patterns on cathode ray tubes.

The whole thrust of this change in the gas station's role from pumping gas to providing complete car care services has been more aimed at convenience than toward increasing car owner awareness of the importance of preventive maintenance. It's easy to fall into the habit of letting Harry's Service take care of everything. The alternatives are to do simple work yourself and shop around for other services. The people who don't involve themselves in their own cars are not enthusiasts in the true sense, and they don't demand the perfection and attention to detail that makes some cars stand out as exceptional pieces of machinery.

Unfortunately for enthusiasts, they are in the minority.

The service industry is not set up to give them what they want when they want it. It's really designed to provide minimum and emergency service for the overwhelming majority of motorists who either don't care or haven't the time to attend to the needs of their personal transportation. To understand how to get the most out of the automotive aftermarket, let's examine how it is organized.

At the retail level, where most of the products and services are sold, the service station is only one of a number of types of outlets. The independent garageman, who used to be the backbone of service and repair, now has to compete with many specialty chains that provide services on more of an assembly line basis. There are the brake, transmission, tire, and diagnostic (tune-up) centers. Every new car dealer network has its own service and parts system, the use of which is encouraged by the factory's warranty contracts; these contracts urge strongly, if they don't actually insist, that car care work be done at an authorized dealership to keep the warranty in effect. Mass merchandisers, such as department stores and discount store chains, have created car care centers that handle most maintenance services except major repairs. For the person who does most of his own work on his car, there are auto supply houses, speed shops, and auto product sections in department and discount stores and even in some supermarkets, plus the parts counters of new car dealerships.

Supplying this variety of retailers are the parts jobbers and warehouse distributors, the modern backbone of the aftermarket. They gather the products of hundreds of manufacturers and distribute them to individual service stations, garages, repair centers, auto supply stores, and speed shops.

The business of maintaining the nation's one hundred million motor vehicles, then, has become a matter of profit seeking by all the people involved in the industry's so-called "supply chain"—from the parts manufacturer to the garage mechanic. The key to how well this network of maker, middleman, and merchandiser serves the public is at the retail level.

The service you get is only as good as the people who provide it, and the problems of the industry are magnified at the place where the customer deals with the serviceman.

First, there is a nationwide shortage of trained automobile mechanics. Cars have become more difficult to work on and have acquired new systems that call for special skills to maintain them, while at the same time fewer young men have been entering the industry. The people who make policy within the aftermarket industry decided some years ago that the best way the customer could be served in this situation was to offer him more bolt-on parts and less "repair" work. This would simplify the task for the mechanic, get the work done more quickly, and provide the service facility owner more profit.

The idea has some merit, although it has helped to inflate the cost of keeping automobiles on the road. It's more expensive to throw away old parts and put new ones on than to try to repair and upgrade the old parts, but there is less chance of making costly mistakes. Spark plugs that used to be cleaned are now discarded and new plugs are put in. Generators that used to be overhauled are replaced.

Tires that need recapping are traded in for new tires. Car owners don't seek out the cause of poor engine performance any more. They take in their cars for a tune-up. Very few people know or even care what is done to their cars to make them work right again.

Even those people who buy new cars and want them to have the best care (and to maintain their warranties) have little idea what work is being performed. The reason many of us suffer the abuses of the repair gyps and the incompetence of mechanics—which cost motorists millions of dollars annually—is that we accept the system as it is. The auto service industry isn't really as bad as it's painted to be, but the average motorist can become dissatisfied, suspicious, and cynical about any dealings he might have with an auto mechanic. Let's not concern this discussion with the isolated examples of out-and-out fraud. Highly sensational exposes make good reading, but they do not solve the more serious weaknesses of the system. Let's look at what happens when the car owner takes his vehicle into the honest shop, the new car agency service department, where the dealer's own integrity and the image of the manufacturer are on the line.

Our car owner is a working man. He is inconvenienced by having to leave his car at the dealership, because he normally uses it to drive to work. He has had to make other arrangements for his transportation that day. His wife or a co-worker will drive him to work, or he will have to use public transportation. So he naturally wants to spend as little time as necessary dropping off the automobile.

When he drives into the service department, he is met

by a man in a white coat with a clipboard. The white coater may call himself a customer service representative or the service manager, or any number of titles, but he is known in the trade as the service writer. Usually, anything he writes on the service order that costs you money will mean a small commission to him. Therefore, he has the incentive to induce the customer to correct as many things wrong with the car as he can. The motorist waits while the man in the white coat writes down the license number and description of the car, checks the odometer, and gets the owner's name, address and phone number. Then he politely asks, "What seems to be the problem?" If the car is there for routine service, he probably will write down something vague, such as "24,000-mile checkup," on the often incorrect assumption that the car owner knows what is going to be done to his car. The service writer will write on the service order anything the motorist wants checked, and the mechanic looks at whatever is written on the order. The motorist can be assured that whatever problem he wants repaired will be done, no matter what the cost. As soon as the service writer finishes filling out the service order, he asks the customer to sign it. At this point the customer has a chance to ask the sort of questions that could save him a lot of money, but he rarely does.

Those questions might include: the cost of a repair; what the alternatives to repair or replacement of parts might be; what type of corrective action might result, depending upon what the mechanic learns from his inspection of the problems; what the problem is already costing the motorist in the car's operation; what procedure the mechanic is

Bondurant instructor Jim Shopneck demonstrates the proper three- and nine-o'clock position for holding the steering wheel.

Proper hand position:
Hands at 3 and 9 o'clock, thumbs hooked over the braces;

Beginning of a left hand turn:
left hand reaches over and hooks thumb under 3 o'clock brace;

Left hand guides wheel over, sliding through right hand, which will grasp opposite brace — and will continue to turn the wheel if necessary.

Below: Shifting: Short smooth movement by right hand to gear lever. As soon as the shift is completed, the hand returns immediately to the steering wheel, never rests on the gearshift lever.

Three foot positions:
Left foot on the Dead Pedal alongside the clutch, right foot on the accelerator;

Left foot on the Dead Pedal, right foot on the brake;

Both feet operating all three active pedals, left foot on clutch for shifting, right foot on brake with heel shifted over to accelerator to raise revs for double clutching maneuver common to downshifts. This position is called heel and toe.

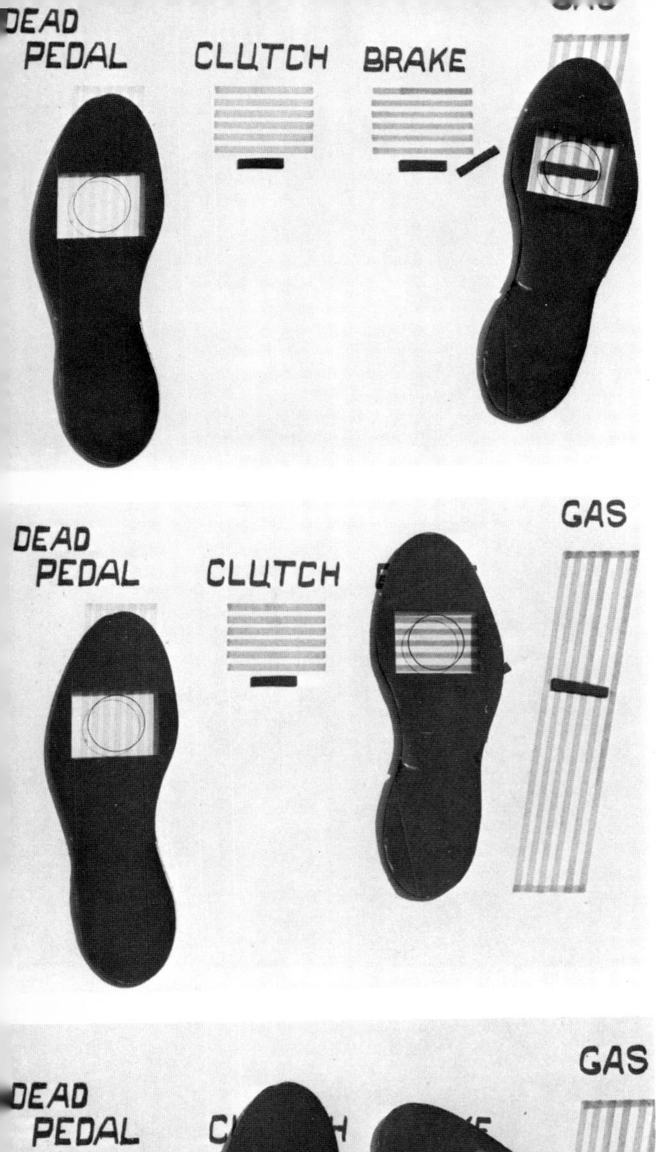

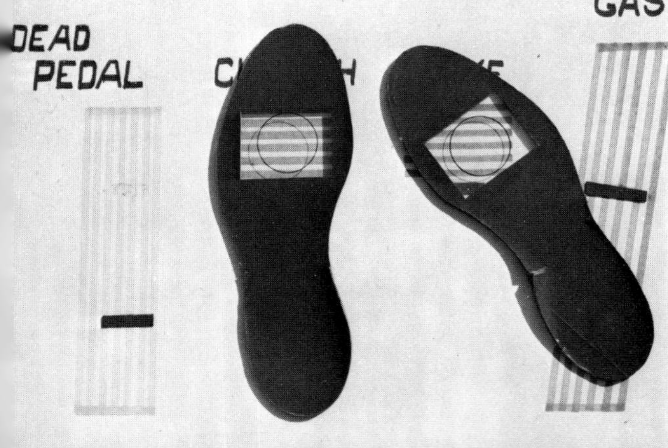

The three maneuvers done in diagram form, the way they are shown in Bob Bondurant's ground school.

Instructor Bob Earl explains proper foot position for heel and toe movement, during ground school. In foreground is model car used on table top to illustrate vehicle dynamics and the proper line through a corner.

Below: Road signs vary from one part of the country to another, and don't always give the driver the kind of information he wants, and expects, to get.

Loading a big camper body onto a pickup truck drastically changes the vehicle's handling characteristics, especially if the truck wasn't ordered with suspension options to accommodate the extra weight. Towing a trailer will only add to this vacationer's problems, even if high speeds and long distances are a normal part of his driving experience.

Learning to avoid someone else's accident, to prevent it from becoming your accident, is not solely for professional race drivers. In fact it is even more important for the average driver than for the racer because the average driver does not have the benefit of a roll cage, safety harness, or helmet.

Bob Bondurant driving an Audi and a Porsche 911 through the same corner, showing the different handling characteristics of front-wheel drive vs. rear-wheel drive.

Bondurant in the classroom explaining the dynamics of staying on the road in a turn.

likely to follow in giving routine service. Chances are, however, the questions will go unasked, and rare is the service writer who will volunteer to give the customer bad news when that information isn't sought. When the customer signs a vague service order, he authorizes all the work and the parts that order calls for. In effect, he is signing a blank check.

Then the car owner goes away, and his car is driven to the service area with the service order attached and assigned to a mechanic. The mechanic, as well as the service writer, normally works on an incentive basis. How to get the work done the best way is left to his discretion, particularly if his instructions are vague. There are two things a mechanic does, one of which he is not paid for. The first task, which he performs for free, is called diagnosis, and the second is known as "R & R," repair and replacement. While he has to contribute his time and muster all his skill and experience to locate the cause of trouble, his pay is determined by how much he can earn under the flat rate pay schedules of "R & R." Almost every repair job a mechanic can perform is covered in a manual which specifies how long the job should take. If it specifies that a certain job normally takes two hours, he will be paid at the flat rate for two hours of work. This is a protection for the customer as well as a guideline to the mechanic, because if the job takes four hours to finish, the customer pays only for two hours of labor in most reputable service establishments.

So the conditions under which the mechanic works make it to his advantage not to spend a lot of time locating problems, but to devote every minute he can to solving them.

Usually, he has a lot of sophisticated diagnostic equipment, such as oscilloscopes, dynamometers, and gauges of every description, to help him reach a quick conclusion, but he shortcuts the diagnostic process whenever possible by taking out "bad" parts and putting in new, good parts. Quite often he does unnecessary work, but he justifies it in his own mind on the basis that the customer eventually would have to replace that part anyway.

If he is a highly skilled mechanic, he can beat the flat rate tables by doing his work in less time than the manual calls for. Good mechanics earn salaries of $20,000 a year and more, and they are worth it. If he is an average mechanic, he still tries to do a conscientious job, but the occasional problem mystifies him, and the easy way out is to replace parts.

For example, fuel pumps and water pumps are frequently replaced, although the trouble is often a clogged line that merely needs cleaning. Ball joints and shock absorbers, according to a panel of General Motors experts, are two of the most frequently over-replaced parts in the automobile's handling package. Rebuilding or overhauling transmissions are sometimes suggested when replacing a bad seal or making a simple adjustment might get the same result. And so on. This approach to the problem of maintenance—throwing away bad parts and putting in good parts to cure the ills of an automobile—does not imply any wrongdoing, but it is a wasteful system, and it sometimes leads to customer dissatisfaction. Some mechanics in the habit of replacing parts without making thorough diagnoses can make wrong guesses and run up the customer's bill without curing his problem.

Some years ago the skilled mechanic used to take the customer's car out and drive it after he was finished with it, to see if everything was working right again. The ultimate test was to drive it up the steepest hill in the neighborhood. A few mechanics still have the time and the opportunity to do that, but conscientious service of that type is the exception now, not the rule. First, court decisions about the responsibilities of service garages and new car agencies who become involved in traffic accidents with customer cars, and the subsequent insurance company reactions, have convinced most people in the business that this level of service has marginal benefit at large risk. Second, mechanics are so swamped with work they don't have time anymore. Very customer-oriented and well-equipped service facilities have a procedure by which the mechanics at least place their cars on the chassis dyno and run them after the work has been done. This dyno testing simulates the drive on the street which the old-time mechanic used to take. In many ways it is more efficient, because the mechanic can "dial in" specific load and speed conditions he needs to test a specific component of the power system. Every minute away from "R & R," however, is a minute of non-productivity, both for the mechanic and for the service department.

Late in the afternoon, after business hours, the car owner returns to pick up his car. The man in the white coat who waited on him in the morning has gone home by now, and when the customer walks up to the service bay to ask about his car he is quickly guided to the cashier window. Inside the cashier's window is someone who has the service order, with dollar amounts all filled in, parts on one side of the order, labor on the other, and a total at the bottom. That total is usually the shock. Routine service, such as the "24,000-mile checkup," can frequently run $90 or more.

To whom can he complain? Who can answer his questions about the work that was done? Why are the charges so high? The cashier doesn't know anything about that part of the transaction. His instructions are not to give up the keys to the car until the customer has paid for the work on the service order. The car owner realizes that he has to pay the bill, but he is left to wonder why routine service has been so expensive.

The reason is that the car owner didn't understand what was going on around him when he came in the door. The cost is so high because he let it be. The maintenance system has grown up around motorists who don't understand the needs of their car and can't be bothered to learn how the system works. A few questions about cost while talking with the service writer in the morning might have saved him a lot of grief later. An admonition to check a problem and call him with the findings of that diagnosis before proceeding would eliminate a lot of the shock he received at the cashier's window.

In addition, when the motorist gets in his car and drives out of the service department, he may or may not be equipped with the mechanical feel to notice right away that not everything was done that should have been. Unfortunately, too many motorists accept 70 or 80 percent performance from their automobiles. They don't have the awareness or "feel" for little things that go wrong.

Little things can mean a lot. A new box of spark plugs may contain a defective plug, often a condition that is undetectable by looking at the fresh plug. However, just one non-firing or mis-firing spark plug put in a V8 engine can mean 12.5 percent power loss. It would mean a 16.7 percent loss in a six-cylinder motor and 25 percent in a four-cylinder.

Even though you're an automotive enthusiast, you may not want to learn auto mechanics and do all the work on your own car, but by taking over some of the simple jobs and by understanding the principles of car care, you can have a better performing, better looking machine, and probably save yourself money at the same time. Let's look at the simple things you can do to take care of your own car with a minimum of investment in time and equipment.

CLEANING

Automobile paint and chrome trim should be washed weekly to keep scum buildup from oxidizing the paint. A car that has been waxed need only be washed with cold water, preferably with a soft chamois cloth to prevent scratching. Once a month the car should be washed with ordinary detergent (soap flakes are less abrasive but don't cut road film as easily) and then waxed. Under ideal conditions a wax job that is not cut by soaping the car's exterior will last longer than a month.

When the car is washed, the interior ought to be vacuumed as well, and seat covers wiped off with a damp cloth. For leather and other fine upholstery, the owner's manual will give cleaning instructions, and if it doesn't, check with an upholstery cleaning establishment and follow its recommendations. Floor carpets should be treated the same as carpets in a home. Approximately once a year they need a rug shampoo treatment if the car is used a lot. The rest of the time a vacuum cleaning will do.

In snow country, exterior car care is a real problem. Left to itself, a car body will rust out in a winter or two. Once rust takes over, it's like cancer. It will rot the body of a car clear through. What gets to the medal quickest is the salt that is picked up by the tires and deposited inside the fender wells. It builds up day after day unless it's removed. There are three choices, none of them perfect remedies, if you want to preserve your treasured automobile. (1) Put it on blocks in the garage for the winter months; (2) undercoat it thoroughly and keep the salt-laden snow from piling up underneath the fenders; or (3) dismantle the rusted parts and replace them when they wear through. No amount of undercoating is going to eliminate rust completely. It will only preserve the metal longer.

For chrome, use special cleaners which you can purchase at any auto supply store and most service stations. It's easier to use steel wool to clean the corrosion off of chrome, but don't give in to the temptation. Steel wool will scratch the chrome plating off more quickly than anything, and then you'll learn how expensive rechroming can be.

Once every six months, depending on local conditions, it's a good idea to steam clean the engine compartment. Not only will the motor clean right up, but if there is anything visibly wrong, such as an oil or water leak, it will be easier to detect after cleaning.

If you're not the type to get out the garden hose and bucket to clean your own car, don't use that excuse to neglect it. There are commercial car washes, and they don't charge very much. For an added fee they will also tend to that steam cleaning chore, and for another they will give you a professional wax job.

Glass is another item that needs attention. When the car is washed, make sure all windows are cleaned on both sides. Road film can easily be washed off the outside, but scum from smoking, normal moisture condensation, and finger painting by children can restrict visibility, and ruin the appearance of an otherwise clean car, too. Windshield wiper blades, whether they are in use or not, wear out and have to be replaced periodically. If you haven't used the wipers recently and a sudden downpour catches you out in the car, make sure they are sweeping properly. If the metal is scraping the window, stop the car and fix the blade or you will have permanent scrape marks on the windshield.

TIRES AND WHEELS

Nothing wears out tires more quickly than letting them run low on air. Two things happen when tires get low. Cornering puts great stress on the sidewalls, and they roll under, multiplying the wear factor, not to mention what it does to handling. At higher speeds excessive friction causes heat buildup, which further weakens the tire casing.

Tire pressures can be adjusted for the desired ride qualities, but if you're not absolutely sure of what you're doing, stick to the manufacturer's specifications.

To begin with, you should exercise care in tire selection and understand the role that tires play in your car's performance. Improvements in tires have accelerated in recent years because of an extraordinary amount of development under racing conditions. Tires are generally wider and lower in profile. They last longer and have different ride characteristics from the old balloon jobs that used to be all the tire manufacturers offered in the replacement market. Both for handling and cosmetics, many drivers of high-performance cars buy oversize tires. Ken Dunipace, the driving performance expert in the National Highway Traffic Safety Administration, views this trend with mixed feelings. He has spent a lot of time researching tires, tire pressures, and their effects on vehicle performance.

"Oversize tires," he says, "make cars handle sharper and corner better. However, some of the oversize tires have rather poor hydroplaning characteristics. In general, I don't think you can say any of these things are always good or always bad, but it is necessary that the guy know what the tradeoffs are. A lot of car owners put these reverse rims on, which change the tread width of the car and the loadings on the wheel bearings. In that case they get some benefit in roll stability and stiffness, but they get added problems of wheel bearing failure. An awful lot of the young kids who do these things are really doing them for appearance and not for performance, anyway. They never stop to think they may be getting some bad effects."

Dunipace explains that this reverse-wheel fad is particularly prevalent among Volkswagen owners who want to dress up their bugs. By mounting their wheels backward they can get them to stick out instead of in. He explains the loading problem that results:

"The accessory manufacturers recognize this as a market and make wheels that are like the reverse wheels, but the lug bolt holes are properly cambered (which is not true of wheels put on in reverse). This widens the tread by three to six inches in some cases. Now, instead of mounting the wheel with a three- or four-inch lever, it's got a six- or eight-inch lever. Obviously, this puts a tremendously greater load on the wheel bearings. Whether this is done by reversing the wheel or with spacers, they both have the same effect."

In changing over from a stock tire to a low profile, wide tread tire, it is highly recommended that you consult a high-performance tire specialist. There is usually one in every large community, and there are any number of specialists advertising in national and regional magazines. While every one of them is interested in selling his own products, they are all performance and safety minded—more so than the local tire dealer who doesn't handle high-performance products—and they will gladly answer requests for information. Some of the better sources for high performance tire information are:

* * *

Carroll Shelby Enterprises (Goodyear), 10930 South La Cienega Blvd., Inglewood, California 90304. Attention: J. L. Henderson.

Parnelli Jones Firestone, 20550 Hawthorne Blvd., Torrance, California 90503. Attention: Marvin Porter.

Post-A-Traction Industries, 622 North La Brea Avenue, Inglewood, California 90302.

Speed Equipment World, 4645 North Central Expressway, Dallas, Texas 75205.

Rodger Ward Performance Tires, 1115 Chestnut Street, Camden, New Jersey 08103.

Universal Imports (Pirelli and Michelin), 14622 Southlawn Avenue, Rockville, New Jersey. (This company offers a tire guide with recommendations for tire pressures and rim widths for $1.)

Semperit of America, Inc., 156 Ludlow Avenue, Northvale, New Jersey 07647.

Mickey Thompson Tires, P. O. Box 227, Cuyahoga Falls, Ohio 44222.

Hi-Performance Tire Company, P. O. Box 4128, North Hollywood, California 91607.

Victory Lane Products (Bobby Unser Tires), 1115 Chestnut Street, Camden, New Jersey 08103.

It is a pleasure to see a car with dress-up wheels and high-performance tires. It is always a sign that the owner of that car cares enough to spend money upgrading it. There are a number of good companies that make wheels for almost any make of car. It is important to check the clearance before making any decision about wheels, because the wrong size wheel can be an expensive mistake. It is also important to check out the product thoroughly if it is to be used in competition. The most reassuring information is whether or not the particular wheel "meets SEMA specs." The Specialty Equipment Manufacturers Association, which also approves other speed equipment according to rigid standards, began examining street and track use of "mag" wheels several years ago after receiving a significant number of failures and complaints from customers. It's hard to get a bad wheel in a speed shop any more, but it is a good sign if that wheel is approved by SEMA's technical committee.

THE COOLING SYSTEM

A good anti-freeze compound will tend to prevent boil over in the summer as well as freezing during the cold weather. However, it is a good policy to drain and flush the radiator twice a year, in the spring and in the fall, to eliminate any corrosion buildup. Most radiators require more care than they normally get. At the first sign of more than a few flecks of rust when you top off the radiator with water, drain it, flush it, and refill. It will help the radiator to last longer and the motor to operate cooler in the long run. The drain plug is easy to locate, and water from the garden hose is pretty cheap.

It's also a good idea to keep an eye on the radiator hoses, hose connections, water pump, fan belts, thermostat, and radiator cap. Maintaining good hoses and belts is the cheapest protection against a seized engine, one that fails because the water cooling system ruptures.

Radiator hoses show excessive wear by bulging or flaking. Have them taken off and thrown away. You can see wear on a fan belt, and if a belt is out of adjustment you can hear it—it will squeal under acceleration.

Water pump replacement used to be a joke. Who hasn't had car trouble in the desert which some unscrupulous mechanic has diagnosed as a leaky water pump? The first time it happened to me many years ago, the transmission blew sixty miles later. Even though water pump sales are a legendary racket, they actually do quit working now and then and need to be watched for telltale signs. All it takes is a visual inspection once in a while. Electrolysis, corrosion, dirt, or other problems do them in.

The engine thermostat controls the circulation of coolant, and in some high-performance cars, signals the fan to switch on or off. Experts say it is over-replaced, but it is difficult for you to tell that you don't need a new one until you replace it. A good rule of thumb is that the fan belt and air flow through the radiator might be the culprit of overheating. They should be checked before the thermostat is replaced. The radiator cap, which pressurizes the cooling system, needs replacing when the rubber gasket inside it begins to leak, releasing the pressure. If the gasket looks okay on inspection, put the cap back on, start the motor, and check the radiator hose for pressure. If it feels firm and not squishy to the touch, the pressure is all right.

THE LUBRICATION SYSTEM

A high-performance automobile needs a high performance motor oil. Preferably, oil with detergents added. The auto maker will specify the ideal weight and some will suggest specific high-grade oils. If your car is older, your mechanic might recommend a heavier grade of oil. It's probably a good idea. Don't wait 6000 miles to change the oil. The modern automobile engine runs a lot hotter than engines did when the oil was supposed to be changed every 3000 miles. Engines have changed, but the oil is still basically the same stuff it has been for millions of years.

Another important factor in the oil system is the filter. Better filters are being made now by several manufacturers. A high-performance engine needs one of these multiple layer filters. We recommend that you select one of the premium filters and change it at the intervals their makers suggest.

THE ELECTRICAL SYSTEM

Everything in the automobile, from the starter to the radio, is dependent on the health of the electrical system. Actually, there are two electrical systems in the car, the ignition system and the one that operates all the accessories. Let's look into the ignition system first.

The process of starting the car begins with the switching on of the ignition and the charge of electricity that is sent to the starter from the storage battery. An electrical impulse passes through the distributor long enough to produce a spark in the spark plugs in each cylinder, which ignites the surge of fuel being sent to the cylinders through the induction system. The interrelation between the ignition and the cam timing engineered into the motor is very critical to the operation of the car.

The four-stroke engine requires that the spark plug ignites the fuel at precisely the same time the piston reaches a point near the top of the cylinder. With four, six, or eight of these pistons all required to contribute to the turning of the crankshaft, it then becomes necessary to coordinate perfectly the timing of the crank and the timing of the spark. Most of this is done by engineering, but the part that needs the most attention is the segment that can be controlled by the mechanic—ignition timing.

The manufacturer lists the precise point on the compression stroke during which ignition should occur. Later model engines, which have lower compression ratios and leaner fuel mixtures, don't always call for the ideal ignition timing setting, but for earlier models they do. Hot-rodders who experiment with their timing, and who change to more exotically engineered cranks, often find an even better setting for the performance of their engines. If you like to experiment with your car's engine, you will find it doesn't take much change in timing to make a big difference in performance. Given a motor with all systems working perfectly, it's the ability to synchronize ignition timing and cam timing at the perfect setting that separates the craftsmen from the mechanics.

There is another variable in the mechanics of timing, the

vacuum spark advance. Obviously, as the speed of the engine increases, the fuel arrives faster on each intake stroke than it did when the engine was running at a slower rate of speed. This quicker delivery is signalled by the carburetor through a diaphragm to the distributor, which then gives orders to each spark plug to alter its firing rhythm slightly in order to accommodate the changes. So timing changes ever so slightly under acceleration, deceleration, high speed running, idle, and so forth. The state of California has seen fit to allow air pollution control devices that switch off this spark advance system in the interest of reducing some pollutants in the exhaust of 1966-1970 automobiles. Learned automotive engineers suggest that these devices adversely affect performance and fuel consumption, and may damage the engine. There is another type of system available to you that may cost more, but which will do the same or even better pollution control job without the potentially bad effects.

Now, the heart of the electrical system is a network of components. Your car's performance will suffer if any single one of them, or any group of them, is not working properly. The car won't run without an alternator (or generator). It will need outside help to start if the battery is run down or if the battery cables aren't transmitting power efficiently. Wiring that is cracked, broken, or exposed due to the wearing away of insulation will leak electricity or even fail. The distributor must be in perfect shape, or it will send the wrong signals to the spark plugs—or perhaps no signals at all. The voltage regulator acts as a sort of traffic cop, making sure the entire system is getting the right amounts of electricity at the right times. And each spark plug controls one-eighth to one-fourth of the power potential of the engine.

Let's look at spark plugs another way. They also control the pollution output of the exhaust. One misfiring or non-firing plug can contribute more auto exhaust pollution than an entire eight-cylinder engine running at full speed without any smog controls. Considering that spark plugs only cost anywhere from seventy-five cents to a few dollars each, it is pretty important to make sure they are not fouling up a $3000 automobile.

Often a plug doesn't need replacing, only cleaning. The service garage philosophy is that fouled plugs should be thrown away and replaced frequently, when actually a good plug should last 10,000 to 15,000 miles if it is kept in good, clean condition and adjusted properly. By learning to care for your own spark plugs, you can do a better job of caring for your car and save money at the same time. It is also a good idea to get in the habit of inspecting your plugs so that you can keep track of how your engine is operating in general.

A used plug that is working well, for instance, will have an insulator tip that varies in color from grayish yellow to brown. That will indicate the charge is flowing properly, the heat in the cylinder is in the proper range, and the exhaust is relatively clean. However, if the plug is black, with a fine film of carbon dust formed on it, either the air/fuel mixture is too rich, the gap is too large, or the plug is too "cold" to burn away deposits. A shiny, cruddy black formation indicates the possibility of a far more serious problem known as "oiling the plugs." It often means the piston rings are worn or the piston is scored, allowing oil to seep into the combustion chamber, but the condition may also be corrected with a hotter plug. Too hot a plug will show up when the insulator tip or the electrode is partially burned away. It may be that the fuel mixture is too lean or the plug wasn't properly installed. Valve leakage might also be the culprit.

The distributor, which regulates the sending of electrical impulses to the plugs through a set of breaker points, will open and close those points 150 million times in 10,000 miles. After those 150 to 200 million openings and closings, they are just about shot and should be replaced.

The distributor and spark plugs, the heart of the system, take the hardest use of any part of the system, but they aren't the only components that show wear. The alternator (or generator), ignition coil, starter, and voltage regulator are the other most frequently replaced parts. To confirm what is causing your car's electrical problem, the quickest and surest way is to take it to a mechanic who knows how to read an oscilloscope properly. The electrical impulse, read out onto a television-like screen through a cathode ray tube, tells its own story. It traces the pattern of each cylinder's firing and shows precisely where the problem lies. It diagnoses illness, and after the "cure" the scope will reveal if the operation performed was a success. Highly skilled veteran mechanics can sometimes listen to a motor and tell what is wrong, but a scope gives the documentation, in living green and white.

You can tell just by looking when some things go wrong—

corrosion of a battery or its connecting cables, for instance. You can easily clean off a battery by sprinkling baking soda on it and dousing it with water. After such a treatment, merely wash it off with water. To prevent corrosion from forming, coat the susceptible spots with grease. It's also a good idea to throw away battery cables that show signs of insulation wear or corrosion, especially around the battery terminals. New cables are cheap. Batteries aren't.

The pesky part of the electrical system that can plague the car owner to death is the part which works everything that is not related directly to the engine. It's also the part that isn't absolutely vital to running the car, and for that reason it's often neglected. Some sports cars are notorious for their shoddy wiring. I owned one of them once, and I wondered if little things kept burning because I wasn't taking proper care of the car, until I learned that the particular wiring loom in my car was frequently subject to failure in cars of the same make. My mechanic, a jovial fellow called Big John, cursed and fumed every time he saw me coming in, until finally he had had enough tinkering with the wiring and tore out the entire system and replaced it. It worked after that, but wow! at great expense to win Big John's good will.

The auxiliary system operates the headlights, taillights, backup lights, brake lights, interior ceiling light, dash lights, and cigarette lighter. It also provides power for anything else that is added on, such as the radio, heater and air conditioner blowers, and stereo system. In some cars it runs the windshield wipers, the push-button windows, fog lights, spotlights, map reading lights and seat adjustment controls.

In the older cars, such as the kind my family drives, one of the lights or control systems is always in need of attention. Every time the car goes in for service, have the little things fixed, or they will spread like cancer and affect the entire system. It has happened more than once to me.

BRAKES

It goes without saying that brakes should always be in good operating condition. Some modern brake systems, however, give little or no warning when they are about to fail. They are self-adjusting. Before self-adjusting brakes became standard, you could tell by the feel of the foot pedal when the brakes became worn. When the brake pedal had to be pushed too far toward the floor, you would go in and have the brakes adjusted, and they would work fine again until the next time for adjustment. Now, every time you back up and put on the brakes, the drum turns a little wheel, adjusting itself. The first time the foot travel increases it could mean the brakes are beyond needing adjustment, and require major overhaul, instead.

There are several other signs that brakes need attention. Brake squeal means there may be dirt on the linings. Brake fade probably indicates the linings are worn. A scratching sound and feel to the brakes means that linings have worn so thin you have started to score them with other brake hardware.

Good brake care starts with using good material. Just as tires should be selected with care because of the role they play in safety and performance, so should brake linings, shoes, and cylinders. If you use premium brake linings and other materials, brakes should last a minimum of 20,000 miles and probably could go longer. But they should be checked every 10,000 miles routinely. The master cylinder should last 50,000 miles under normal conditions, but it should be monitored routinely.

It's not recommended that you do your own brake maintenance unless you are skilled, but you can do your own inspection by pulling each wheel and making visual examinations. If you have to pull a wheel for any reason, always check the brakes.

HANDLING PACKAGE

This includes the suspension and steering systems. Rear suspension is critical for applying power to the road and supporting the weight of the car, while the front suspension is vital to steering and braking.

Most cars on the road use the conventional "live" axle in the rear. It houses the differential in the center and the wheels and brakes are attached to the outer extremities. The axle is supported either by leaf springs or coils.

Some suspension systems are fully independent, but independent axles are most likely to be found only in the front. Except for expensive sports cars, the only typical independent rear suspensions are found on the VW bug, which has a swing axle. The differential is mounted on the frame of the VW and the drive is given to the wheels through pivoting axle shafts. Some foreign cars offer a semi-trailing arm rear suspension, particularly those with front-drive layouts.

The front suspension of most cars on the road is independently sprung, by means of A-arms. The front wheels pivot in place to accomplish the turning, which places a great deal of the dynamic stress on the front assembly. That's why it is possible to achieve better traction during a high-speed cornering maneuver by continuing to brake while turning, bringing more weight to bear on the pivoting front wheels.

Tying together the road-holding package are the shock absorbers, which are designed to cushion the bumps taken by the tires and transmitted to the suspension; shock absorbers also help secure the chassis when it wants to wander.

Then there is the anti-roll torsion bar, which increases roll stiffness under dynamic stress; it is usually in the front suspension system, but in some cars at the rear.

The entire complex network of springs, bars, struts, axles, steering points, and pivots should be cared for with regular lubrication and inspection. Steering systems in passenger cars are designed to last the life of the car, even under hard use. High-speed driving on bad surfaces over a long period of time, however, will tear up a steering assembly just as easily as it will damage shock absorbers and axles.

Consumer advocates claim that unscrupulous mechanics will try to sell you ball joints when they get your car up on the rack, because when the car is off the pavement the wheel can be moved to "prove" it is loose, when in fact it is *always* loose without weight on it. Visual inspection will show real wear. The second most over-sold item, consumerists say, is the shock absorber. Again, you can tell when the shocks are in need of replacement. If you hit a bump and the car continues rocking or pitching long after it has recovered from the shock, the shock absorbers are worn or maybe even broken. You can test shocks by leaning hard on the front or rear of the car. When you let go it should rise to its normal position. If it continues bouncing up and down several times, the shocks need replacing.

Most shimmying, wheel bouncing, and other frightening responses of the car can be cured by wheel balancing, which is inexpensive. If a wheel is out of balance it can easily be detected with simple testing at a front-end repair station or at a tire store. Another more drastic repair is front-end alignment. The earliest sign of the need for either wheel balance or alignment is uneven tire wear. Except for excessive wear in the center of the tread, which usually means over-inflation, any uneven tread wear, inside, outside, or undulating, means the car probably needs either wheel balancing or front-end alignment. Always check first to make sure the wheels are balanced. If you are in the market for improving the handling package on your car, most sports car manufacturers offer special suspension kits. If you aren't sophisticated in this area, the best advice is to consult a good high-performance mechanic who is acquainted with your type of car. Don't tell him what to do, tell him what you want to achieve and then listen. He'll tell you if it can be done, and if it can't, don't try it. You might end up spending a lot of money on something that won't make your car handle any better and may even make a dog out of it.

In general, front anti-roll bars increase roll stiffness, if that is desired, but stiffer springs often deteriorate the ride quality on rough roads. High-performance shocks may not make a great deal of difference in the handling of your car, but they will last a lot longer and after even extreme wear will deteriorate at a slower rate. If the premium racing-type shocks are too expensive, the least you can do is put heavy-duty shock absorbers on the car. One type of racing suspension we strongly recommend against is the so-called hi-lifter. For the drag strip it provides a little advantage in acceleration, and if that is the only place it is used, it is desirable. But anything you gain in redistributing the weight for drag racing is more than offset by ill handling in braking and cornering. A drag racing fan can see this on almost any given Saturday night. When Funny Cars, which are grotesquely canted upward in the rear, do their burnouts they sway dangerously under braking. Ditto Pro Stocks.

THE POWER TRAIN

While the motor operates to turn a crankshaft, this twisting motion has to be translated somehow into making the automobile move. This is done by the least understood of its components, the transmission and differential.

The transmission connects the crankshaft with the drive shaft. The twisting of the drive shaft, however, must be converted to driving power at the wheels, and this is where the differential goes to work. In this process, the power train actually carries the work of the engine to the driving wheels and changes the application of twisting motion, or torque, from the front-to-back position of the engine shaft to the side-to-side rear axle.

Accelerating the car from dead stop to full speed ahead is also made easier by the transmission, because it carries the engine's output through a series of gears. If two gears of the same size are meshed to rotate two separate shafts, they will revolve at the same speed. But if the driving gear is one-third the size of the driven gear, the driven gear will revolve only one-third as fast as the driving gear. In this condition the driving gear is able to apply a lot of torque, which is needed to move the automobile off from a standing start. This small vs. large combination is called first gear.

As momentum is increased less torque is needed. So the next set of gears is a combination in which the driven gear is reduced in size and the driving gear is larger. This change in sizes continues until the two gears are equal in size when the shafts are united in top gear, which is usually third or fourth, and in some racing cars can be fifth or even sixth gear.

To enable these gears to mesh with the least amount of clashing, the clutch acts as a middleman. It enables the engine to run, turning the crankshaft, while the transmission remains disconnected. In a manual transmission this is done when the driver pushes in the clutch pedal. This separates the two plates of the clutch, which prevents the engine from spinning the gears in the transmission, and allows the driver to shift. As the driver releases the clutch pedal, the clutch plates come together and reconnect the engine to the transmission.

Theoretically, in top gear the driveline is turning at the same speed as the engine shaft, but there is a reduction in ratio that takes place in the differential, which must translate the rotation of a narrow shaft to the turning of much larger wheels. This reduction is called the final drive ratio. Rear-end gearing can approach 1 to 1, but very rarely does. It generally ranges between 3 to 1 and 4 to 1, that is, three or four revolutions of the drive shaft for every one revolution of the driving wheels.

In the automatic transmission a fluid coupling replaces the clutch. Hydraulic pressure, which acts on the oil bath inside the transmission casing, is controlled by car speed and throttle opening, and engages the gears automatically. When the engine turns, oil is thrown onto the driven member (turbine) by the driving member (impeller), and the driveline is turned.

There are two methods of gearing to provide the high torque needed at low speed, and to tone down the torque at cruising speed. One is based on the torque converter principle, which is used to multiply torque. Between the impeller and the turbine a third member, called a stator, is introduced. It catches oil which has been pumped against the turbine and diverts it so that it doesn't flow back into the path of other oil being pumped at the turbine. As speed increases, the stator does less work. The other system is a complex series of planetary gears, clutches, and hydraulics which provide three forward speeds, neutral, and reverse.

Together, the torque converter and the planetary transmission provide the drive train with an almost unlimited combination of torque and speed settings.

In caring for a manual transmission, which may be the most rugged single component of the drive system, the most important thing you can do is practice smooth driving. Sudden clutch popping, gear grinding, radical downshifting, and lugging exact a heavy toll on clutch and gear life. Smoothness is the best technique to get good lap times on the road course and at the same time baby the transmission. On the drag strip, too, smoothness pays. Precious hundredths of seconds are lost when gears don't mesh properly due to a sloppy, hurried shift. Should gears wear, they can be replaced at less than exorbitant prices, although the labor bill may be high. Ordinarily, if the transmission stays lubricated properly, and if it is not abused by the driver, it will last the serviceable life of any car.

Oil in the automatic transmission plays a very important role in its operation. It is usually recommended that it be changed and the filter be replaced every 24,000 miles, but under hard usage you will probably want to change it more often. Heat is the biggest enemy of transmission oil. If you drive a lot in hot weather, you should change it as often as every 12,000 miles.

Just as frequently, check the level and color of the fluid in the differential. A little fresh lubrication is a lot less expensive than a rear axle overhaul. The differential is also subject to a lot of abuse on rough roads, since it is driving the wheels, which are bouncing, and it is being bounced around considerably as well. Linkages to the differential will show wear and should be examined the first time any strange noises begin emanating from the rear end. These linkages are the universal joints, which should be lubricated at least every 24,000 miles and examined carefully at that time. While the rear-end housing is off, a visual inspection can be made of the gears at the same time. For normal street driving this much care isn't usually necessary, but in racing—where quick-change rear ends are exchanged often in minutes to meet track conditions—rear axles are examined constantly. Depending on your type of driving, take counsel from that.

INSTRUMENTS

Most modern cars, except for some sports cars, provide inadequate instrument packages. Spend $4000 to $5000 on a new automobile and what do you get on the dashboard? The speedometer, on which you can't depend until you have it caliberated at your own personal expense, the odometer, a gas gauge, sometimes a water temperature meter, and a set of colored lights that go on at various times.

New safety regulations have added a series of "idiot-proofing" lights and buzzers that glow and honk their contempt for the average motorist. One is a message that tells you the brake is still on, another an admonition to fasten your seat belt. In later models an annoying buzzer persists until you either belt up or extend the male side of the belt and sit on it to shut off the sound. In some cars a flashing red light tells you that the door isn't properly closed.

There is more of this insulting gadgetry in the offing, and considering the nation's safety record some of it isn't a bad idea. One gimmick is attached to the ignition system, and it requires that you perform a mechanical function, such as punching out a series of numbers on a console before starting the car. The theory is that it is simple enough for anyone to do—if he's sober. Drunk, he messes up the job and the car won't start.

Back when Henry Ford was producing the Model T he gave the operator an amperage meter and even let him retard the spark manually with a lever so he could start the car easier. Most of the logic behind simplifying the dashboard (and controls) has been the industry's cynical view that the motorist doesn't really pay attention to instruments anyway, so why provide them unless he demands them? Any stylist or engineer trying to justify this position can cite the frequency that drivers let their cars run out of fuel—and except for some early model Volkswagens nearly every car on the road has a fuel gauge.

It is interesting to note that race cars have few instruments, but that the ones they have are more functional than those found on the average street-legal automobile. The most important is the tachometer, which measures engine speed. Very few race drivers have speedometers installed, because they don't need to know how fast they are going. Those who do are merely curious, or else they are driving vehicles that once were operated on the street and they didn't bother to disconnect the speedo. It may be difficult to believe, but many race cars don't even have a fuel gauge. If their type of racing doesn't require a fuel stop they would have no reason ever to look at the fuel level, and so they leave the fuel capacity meter off the dash on the theory that it is one less thing to have to look at during a race. One instrument found in most race cars, however, is a fuel pressure gauge. It's seldom needed except for emergencies, when the car stops running well. The driver can check fuel pressure and assign the blame to the fuel system, if that's where the problem lies, when he makes an unscheduled pit stop the next time around. Two very important functional instruments found in nearly all race cars are oil pressure and temperature gauges. When oil pressure drops suddenly, the wise race driver shuts off his ignition and coasts to a stop. Oil temp is a better gauge of interior engine heat than water coolant temperature, which can be modified by the thermostat, and when oil temperature rises above normal the smart driver slows down to save his engine.

On the street, instrumentation should be adequate to your use of a car. There are many fine gauges on the market which give you a better idea of how your car is operating.

With a manual transmission a tachometer is useful to prevent over-revving in each of the gears. An oil pressure gauge is another worthwhile purchase, if one isn't provided with the car. Often oil pressure can be reduced, but not enough to show up as almost no pressure at all, which is the condition necessary to switch on the red oil pressure warning light. Gradually receding pressure may not be a serious problem, but it could bear watching. The oil pump may need replacing or it may be clogged with dirt. Lower oil pressure might be a signal of low oil level. An oil pressure gauge will give warning before the oil pressure gets to the disaster level of near zero. When the red light goes on it's too late to do anything but park and wonder how much damage has been done. An amperage meter is also useful, because it often tips off the driver when he has problems that wouldn't show up right away with the red light that indicates discharge. When the needle flops well over into the charge zone, it means the battery is accepting a lot of power for storage, which in turn means it has used a lot. The battery may be wearing out or there may be a short somewhere in the system that has caused the battery to run down. A slight discharge signals that the alternator may not be running properly. A needle right on neutral or a shade to the charge side usually indicates the electrical system is doing fine.

It is even possible to buy such sophisticated gadgetry as a dwellmeter for your dash, but that has to be a personal decision, because little purpose other than curiosity can be served. For rallyists there are computer packs that measure mileage and estimate speeds quite precisely, and digital clocks for super accurate timing. The choice is the consumer's. Much of what is on the market is cosmetic, but only you know precisely the need for instruments in your own high-performance car.

7

So You Want to Be a Race Driver?

There are more than eight hundred motor racing facilities in the United States. The figure is probably closer to a thousand, but nobody has counted them yet with any degree of accuracy. If you were to confine your attention to automobile-type racing alone, you would also be astounded with the variety of competition there really is. It seems as if everything man has put a motor in he has figured out how to race. There are:

Drag racing, including street, stock, modified production, competition coupe and sedan, altered, dragster, pro stock, and funny car. Stock car racing, including hardtop, mini-stock, sportsman, hobby, compact, modified, limited, late model, new model, Grand National, and Grand American "baby grand." Midget racing, including quarter-midgets, half-, micro-, three-quarter-, modified-, and just plain ordinary midget-midgets. Open wheel modified and winged supermodified racing. Road racing, including sedan, production sports car, GT, touring car, formula, sports/racing car, and Can-Am racing. Off-road and ATV racing. Snowmobile and ice racing. Solo speed events. Hill climbs and sand drags. Rallying. Championship car racing on oval and road course. Dirt cars. And more.

Each division of motor racing has its many variations, and almost everywhere you go there are separate associations which have rule variations that make their particular kind of racing unique. As a hobby it's expensive, but it's available.

In some parts of the country you can start at the age of five in a quarter-midget. Practically everywhere you can start when you are old enough to hold a valid driver's license, in some form of racing. All but a few associations allow eighteen-year-olds to compete. There are still holdouts, notably the U. S. Auto Club (USAC), which insist on their drivers being twenty-one years old. With the advent of eighteen-year-old voting rights, even these age barriers are not absolute. They might be expected to change with the times in due course.

In addition to age, sex is becoming less of a barrier to participation in racing. Where the bars are not lowered voluntarily, eager young women racing aspirants have sought relief through the courts in several ways and have generally been successful. One method has been to file an action under the Fair Employment Practices Act, as one Tacoma, Washington, lass did against a motorcycle racing club. Another has been to sue for damages and injunctive assistance under the due process guarantees of the U. S. Constitution's Bill of Rights.

There is a serious question about the physical limitations of women in certain types of racing that require great strength and endurance, should women be allowed to race against men. However, as the right to equal opportunity is extended to women at one race track after another, the distinctions seem less important. What could be more physically or mentally demanding than a 12- or 24-hour endurance road race, with all its dangers as well as the brain-numbing factor of fatigue? Yet, women have driven race cars successfully and almost without incident at Sebring and Daytona, Le Mans and Nurburgring.

Women have been accepted in road racing since the early post-war days here and in Europe. Drag racing has welcomed them in the stock and street classes since the sport was born, and in recent years has encouraged female superstars in funny car, fuel dragster, and pro stock classes reserved almost exclusively for the top touring professionals. There has seldom been a question of women competing at the amateur or semi-pro levels in other racing, but they have been banned from USAC and effectively excluded from major NASCAR (National Association for Stock Car Auto Racing) events with few exceptions.

The most notable is Paula Murphy, who drove her way from the "ladies' race" of the California Sports Car Club (SCCA) through jalopies, record runs at Bonneville, and a factory ride on the Mobil Economy Run to a career as a funny car driver and the distinction of being one of the few licensed rocket car drivers in the world. Her precedent breaking in drag racing, which became successful only after she threatened to sue NHRA (National Hot Rod Association), opened the door to women in all fuel-burning race car competition. Paula also lapped Indianapolis Motor Speedway in one of the cranky old STP Novis during a tire test, with the knowledge and approval of USAC officials, to break the all-male tradition of that somewhat hidebound racing organization. She later lapped in a Grand National stock car at Talladega to set a closed course Land Speed Record and lay yet another feminine prohibition to rest.

Should women ever become interested in auto racing as participants on a grand scale, they will probably prove that they are as capable of managing themselves in a racing car as a man, but until then most enthusiasts of the sport will continue to theorize that they are just not physically equipped to handle big time racing. Women are not now prevented in theory from advancing their careers in professional race car driving, only in practice.

With the exceptions just noted, you can get into just about any type of racing if you are physically able to qualify, either own the equipment or have it available to you and meet the other simple requirements of the association you have to join to get started.

MIDGET RACING

Quarter-midget racing was the rage in the 1950s. It started when Doug Caruthers, a manufacturer in Anaheim, California, and the Indianapolis racing star, Jimmy Bryan, built a track next to Doug's factory for his two youngsters, Jimmy and Danny. They had already built the older boy a midget race car in the off-season and decided that five-year-old Jimmy needed a track to run his car on. So they got out one weekend with a bulldozer and carved out a one-tenth-mile oval next to the company parking lot. When the youngster tried the car out on the track one Sunday, he created a monumental traffic jam on Manchester Boulevard, as Sunday-driving motorists became curious and stopped to have a look at the strange sight. Two weeks later there were several other fathers and their boys out to run their home-built cars on the track. That started Doug Caruthers to thinking: He might have stumbled into something big.

So Doug Caruthers went into the business of manufacturing quarter-midgets and promoting the sport. For a while there were quarter-midget races for kids everywhere. The sport made national television (on the "Mickey Mouse Show" and "Art Baker's House Party," to name two programs), and soon there were national championships and a whole structure of rules and procedures. Doug Caruthers began manufacturing the cars according to the racing formula he had devised. He went to USAC with the idea that it undertake to supervise quarter-midget racing much in the same way Little League baseball was managed, but the proposal was turned down. The Caruthers boys were among several professional racing drivers who got their first exposure in a quarter-midget. Some of the others were Johnny Parsons, Swede Savage, Bruce Walkup, and Pancho Carter.

With the advent of the mini-bike, and mini-bike racing, the popularity of quarter-midgets has waned, but there are still scattered associations that provide competition for grade school aged youngsters, boys and girls, up to the age of twelve.

KART RACING

At the age of eight a youngster can move into sprint kart racing, although he (or she) will be allowed to race only in the underpowered four-cycle class. At his twelfth birthday, he becomes eligible for enduro karting. Go-kart racing was another fad sport that has lost some of the popularity it enjoyed in this country in the late 1950s and early 1960s. But there is still a strong cadre of enthusiastic supporters from coast to coast and an organizational structure that oversees everything from local meets to national championships. From time to time the top American drivers even travel to foreign countries for invitational meets.

There is no age limit for karting, and the various levels of competition enable beginners to compete comfortably, while the virtual pros in the sport can race with each other in the safe knowledge that novices are not likely to get in the way.

The two basic types of karting are quite different. Sprint kart races are held on small, very twisting courses, smaller and narrower than slalom tracks and practically without straightaways. They seldom grow to more than three-quarters of a mile in length. Because they are so tight, they are the ultimate tests of kart handling and driver skill at lower speeds in heavy traffic. Enduro karting, on the other hand, is done on regular championship road courses, from Watkins Glen to Riverside, Road Atlanta to Elkhart Lake. Speeds reach as high as 120 miles an hour, and the best kart drivers can come reasonably close to lap times of much more powerful sports cars, because they are able to fly through the corners flat out.

Kart racing is a good place for a teenager to find out if he has the aptitude and the desire for road racing. Swede Savage, Johnny Parsons, and Mike Mosley all were graduated from the quarter-midgets to karts when they reached twelve years of age.

For information about the sport of karting, write:

International Kart Federation
733 East Edna Place
Covina, California 91723

DRAG RACING

In most states the legal age for getting a license to drive on the street is sixteen. If you have a valid operator's license and you apply to one of the major associations, you can go drag racing. On grudge racing nights, usually during midweek, many strips do not even insist that you belong to a recognized organization. Aside from a driver's license, there is only one other requirement, that you have a car in acceptable safety condition. In the case of street classes of cars, this would include being street-legal, but sixteen-year-olds can even hold competition licenses to drive fuel burning, 200 mph dragsters and funny cars under certain conditions. Billy (The Kid) Scott, now a stock car driver, NHRA national champion Jeb Allen, and young

Rich Stewart, who beat Don Garlits the first time he ever faced him, were all sixteen when they acquired their pro licenses from NHRA.

The original intent of making a sport out of drag racing was to give potential street racers a safe place to run their cars. Therefore, youngsters are not only accepted but encouraged to compete. There are three major drag racing associations, each with its official publication to keep members in touch with its activities and its own set of technical and safety rules. To make inquiries write to the following (club publication is also listed, in parentheses):

National Hot Rod Association
10639 Riverside Drive
North Hollywood, California 91602 *(National Dragster)*

American Hot Rod Association
11030 Granada Lane
Overland Park, Kansas 66211 *(Drag World)*

International Hot Rod Association
P. O. Box 3029
Bristol, Tennessee 37620 *(IHRA Drag Review)*

STOCK CAR RACING

In every community of any size there is an oval track where usually at least once a week there is some form of stock car racing. Stock cars represent a broad general class of competition automobiles, ranging from open-wheel hot rods and modified roadsters to jalopies to hobby, sportsman, and late model stocks. The largest and most important stock car association nationally, NASCAR, provides competition clear down through the so-called hobby class, which is set down in the rule books to be an inexpensive class of racing with motors that are not capable of generating very much speed. In the hobby class drivers learn the basics of racing while staying out of speed ranges that could get them in trouble until they acquire the necessary experience. Hobby class rules vary from track to track. West coast rules call for six-cylinder engines with piston displacement up to 250 cubic inches, but in some parts of the country V8 engines are allowed.

The NASCAR system, loosely copied by many other stock car associations, is very much like the competition structure of the American Motorcycle Association that NASCAR's executive vice-president, Lyn Kuchler, used to supervise. It provides for an orderly progression of drivers from one class up to another until he reaches the super-speedway class on the Grand National circuit.

The first step up from hobby cars is into the late model sportsman division. Sportsman stocks are generally cars of the ten model years immediately ahead of Grand National (current three model years) cars, although the precise definition varies from track to track. After 1971, when under this guideline 1957 model cars would have slipped out of the sportsman class, the rules were stretched at many tracks. The reason was that 1957 was a vintage year for racing stock cars, a season when Ford and Chevrolet built racing chassis into their production cars. There was naturally a lot of resistance to the idea that '57 Fords and Chevys had to be retired, and rules allowed 1957s at many places for years after they technically were no longer late model sportsman stock cars.

To call sportsman stocks "early models" in most cases is to do them an injustice. Quite often sportsman stock cars are former Grand National cars and usually they are beautifully kept up. Considering the entire automobile population of the public roads they are probably more representative of stock automobiles being driven by the fans in the stands than Grand National cars are.

Not always, but usually, sportsman class drivers make their next move upward in racing to the Grand National class. NASCAR has regionalized Grand National racing so that there are three circuits for competitors, the Grand National championship series familiarly known to television viewers and patrons of the superspeedways, and two others which are contested mostly on short tracks—Grand National East and Grand National West.

NASCAR has another catch-all division for modified stock cars. These can be older vehicles, and as the name implies they are highly modified. Rules vary from one track to another, so that a modified vehicle might be a pre-World War II coupe in one part of the country and a caged sprint car with a wing on top in another. Wheels are covered or uncovered. The bodies are coupe or sedan. Engine size and setback rules vary. Carburetion types are different.

NASCAR rules allow sixteen-year-olds to race in any division, but as a general rule it takes several years for a newcomer to get the experience necessary to get into the elite of Grand National racing. When he was sixteen, young

Johnny Parsons competed in Grand National West races, or as the division was called at the time, Pacific Coast NASCAR Late Model Division. Richie Panch, son of another famous race driver, Marvin Panch, started racing a sportsman at sixteen and was a Grand National driver at eighteen. NASCAR depends to a great deal on the judgment of its officials and, in fact, has fewer difficulties with accrediting drivers for its various divisions than most racing associations, even though it has fewer formal guidelines.

Outside of NASCAR, there are a host of other stock car sanctioning bodies. In scope they are national, such as USAC's stock car division, regional, such as the Auto Racing Club of America based in the midwest, and local bodies. There are many variations of the early-middle, early-late and early-early model stock racing car with designations that mean different things in different places. There are coupes, roadsters, jalopies, hardtops, sedans, foreign stocks—the names are endless. Rules are rather informal and loosely enforced at many tracks. I know of some drivers who got started with local associations as young as fifteen, but not officially. They had to lie about their ages.

A far more serious and rigid set of rules will govern the young driver's equipment. Although the beginning driver is not likely to run into the exacting sort of technical inspection practiced by NASCAR Grand National scrutineer Bill Gazaway at every short track in the country, the novice is going to face a tough barrier to racing at tech. The most important document a rookie can get his hands on is a set of the rules. The most important section of the rule book is the one that deals with safety features of the driver's equipment.

A veteran official once told me that drivers try to cheat on the stupidest, least productive items in racing, the rules dealing with the safety of their own lives.

"If you don't watch the drivers closely," he said, "they would climb into their cars and race in T-shirts."

A flameproof driving suit makes good sense. It doesn't make a racer any slower or any faster, only safer. If you are planning to enjoy racing for any length of time, the best mental approach is to accept safety restrictions and not try to take shortcuts around them.

Most technical inspectors—in fact most racing officials and a large number of competing veteran drivers—dealing with rookies, take a helpful attitude. They know the sport is complex and confusing to the beginner, and they remember how it was when they got started. If you have a question, it isn't always necessary to wait until you get out to the race track. If you ask for a special ruling, an inspector will often come over to your racing shop. When you get to the track and learn you have made a mistake on some safety item, you will often find friendly advice and helpful hands to assist you in making corrections.

The safety part of the inspection process is the most important part, but the other segment deals with rules that define the particular kind of racing you are doing. It is supposed to detect and prevent cheating. New drivers are seldom suspected of shady practices, and their lack of experience usually prevents them from "interpreting" the rule book. Cheating, of course, is damnable, but making intelligent use of rules to benefit yourself is called ingenuity. One of the important talents a racer can develop is the ability to create "speed secrets" that conform to the letter of the rules. The best time to begin developing that talent is right at the beginning. That means it is essential that you learn to read a rule book and understand the rules thoroughly at all times.

For more information about NASCAR, write:

National Association for Stock Car Auto Racing, Inc.
P. O. Box K
Daytona Beach, Florida 32015

ROAD RACING

The Sports Car Club of America, which was one of the major institutions holding the line on its driver licensing at a twenty-one-year age minimum, changed its rules in 1972 to allow eighteen-year-olds to compete on a limited basis. It was the most significant change in attitude toward accrediting drivers since sports car racing became a professional sport in the 1960s.

SCCA governs most of the road racing done in this country, which means that it regulates nearly every type of automobile that can be raced on a twisting road course—formula cars, production sports cars, sports/racing cars, sedans (they're called saloon cars in England), and showroom stock sedans. This supervision begins at the level where most beginners get their first exposure to road racing

—solo events—and blankets everything up to and including Formula 1.

To get started in SCCA it is necessary to join both the national club and a local region of SCCA. The national membership fee is $17.50, which includes a subscription to the club's national magazine, *Sports Car,* and makes you eligible for such benefits as group health and life insurance and discounts on products. SCCA reports it is developing a group auto insurance policy to provide its members with even more annual savings. Dues for membership in a local region range from $5 to $10 a year, and they usually entitle the member to receive the region's publication, anything from a newsletter to a slick magazine with national and even international racing coverage and feature articles.

It is possible to sample some forms of competition without joining SCCA. Many local sports car clubs and enthusiast groups stage such events as slaloms, traloms, gymkhanas, autocrosses, and rallies, which are low-speed events that demand a great deal of driver skill without creating undue risk for the car or driver. Getting interested in slalom racing is what launched George Follmer's career. His first competition was in the Volkswagen he used to drive to work. The logical progression from this level is into SCCA's solo event program, which is quite similar but has an additional level of skill requirement in some high-speed events that carry with them hazards not common to everyday driving.

The simplest of these solo events are called Solo II. These are the non-speed, one-car-at-a-time contests, such as slaloms and gymkhanas. They don't require shoulder harnesses or roll bars. The emphasis is on correctly negotiating a tricky, twisting, narrow course without leaving the prescribed path in the shortest possible elapsed time. Along the way there may be special tasks to perform, such as backing up, parking, or making a 360-degree turn inside a turning basin.

Solo I events are also one-car-at-a-time, but they require safety equipment, such as roll bars and harnesses, because mistakes can cause accidents. The most popular Solo I activity is the hill climb. It's a sort of drag race with turns in it, because the winner is the driver who takes the least amount of time from the bottom of the hill to the top. There are also time trials, which are speed events on road courses, often the same courses where racing is conducted. As each additional element of danger is added, the more driving experience is demanded. To graduate from one phase to another is a practical way to ease into road racing, the ultimate speed experience.

There is, however, one intermediate phase of competition that has its own gradations of risk—the elapsed time rally. In simple form the rally is like a treasure hunt. The driver and his navigator follow a simple set of instructions, traveling from one point to the next at prescribed speeds, always at or under the speed limit, on public roads. The object is to prevent getting lost and to arrive at designated checkpoints with as little error in predicted or prescribed elapsed time as possible. Rallies get more sophisticated when the driver/navigator team graduates from the "fun run" class and concentrates on serious competition, such as SCCA provides with its divisional and national championship rallies. The most difficult and most dangerous is the European-type rally. SCCA has one of these, an event which counts in points scored toward the world rallying championship. It is the Press On Regardless Rally in central and northern Michigan, practically an off-road race over some of the toughest terrain in middle America. The most famous of world class rallies, of course, is the Monte Carlo, held in wintertime over different snow and ice-covered roads from various starting points in Europe. World championship rallies are so close to road racing that the distinction is difficult to make. In some of them, different exercises are conducted en route. These include hill climbs, time trials, and even short races.

SCCA conducts formal driver training schools for its fledgling race drivers. The purpose of the schools is not to teach the drivers how to go fast, but how to conduct themselves safely on the road course. SCCA is the only major racing organization which has originated its own formal driver training program, and because of the way the school is set up it gives the rookie driver a better understanding of the overall operation of a race. He is purposely exposed to the role carried out by flagmen, emergency workers, officials, and communications personnel. The instruction includes lectures, chalk talks, walks with the instructor around the course, riding with the instructor around the course, driving with the instructor as a passenger, soloing with observers watching at every turn, and post-soloing evaluations of the student's performance. As a graduation exercise there is even a novice race. All during this process officials of the club are watching, not only the student's driving performance and his conformity to the rules of competition, but also his attitude. A student who does not seem to be paying attention will have a tougher time getting his card signed off at the end of school than his classmates.

Chances are that a lot of the officials working on the race course for the training school will also officiate at the novice driver's early races, and they will be especially careful in watching his performance during a race if they had a bad impression of him in school.

There is another important factor, the student's car. It has to be prepared for racing, as stated in the rules, and it should be carefully set up so that it doesn't break down for any reason. Nobody in SCCA driver's school makes allowances for a DNF ("did not finish"—failure to complete the race.) If the car won't run, you don't get to complete the required six hours of driving over two separate weekends, and in some cases that will mean long delays in completing the training required before you can enter your first race. It might cost you a whole year of competition.

SCCA has recently adopted a friendly and cooperative attitude toward the Bondurant school and some other professional race-driving courses of instruction, considering that experience when a former student applies for a novice license. SCCA still reserves the right to put graduates of such courses through its own driver training school, because officials contend that there is no better place for the beginning racer to be exposed to technical inspection, registration, entry form preparation, racing in traffic, and the officials' control signals.

"Some of these schools give better training than others,"

a spokesman for SCCA said, pointing out that the club particularly likes the Bondurant curriculum.

After completing the required SCCA training, all novices go through an intermediate stage where they are permitted to compete in regional races but can't earn a full regional license right away. They earn this after they complete two races as novices and turn in their novice logbook for a full regional card. Ordinarily, DNFs don't count. If, in the opinion of the chief steward, the driver had the full benefit of experience in the race, even though he didn't finish, this requirement can be waived. A novice's two races can also be shortcutted if he has prior experience in some other form of racing—stock cars, midgets, even karts, if he is particularly talented. The presiding officials, either the chief steward of the SCCA school or the divisional licensing representative, can waive some requirements if the driver shows exceptional ability, even though he has no previous racing experience. But if you are like the rank and file of novices, you must run the two required races, finish them, and have the novice logbook signed off to earn the right to compete in regional championship races.

For you to get the regional license, you request the regional executive to sign off the novice log and send that, along with a medical form and $5, to the SCCA National Headquarters in Denver. The medical form is available at all regions and should be completed by any M.D. you choose to give you a simple physical examination. If you're over forty, the physical exam requirement is a little stiffer, calling for an electro-cardiogram test, in addition to the other steps in the physical. The regional license permits you to race in regional championship events anywhere in the U. S., and after four of them are recorded in your logbook you are eligible to submit the signed-off log, fill in the back of the license with your race finishing records, and send with another $5 filing fee to SCCA to exchange for a national license. After four national SCCA championship races you go through the same process again to apply to SCCA in Denver for an FIA license. The difference this time is that the FIA license requires a $20 filing fee.

A new driver evaluation procedure is followed by SCCA to keep track of the records of its competitors. Every driver must maintain his own logbook and present it at each race. After the race, the chief steward or a designated official must enter the results and make any comments about the driving performance of the individual. Accidents, problems, incidents on the course, and other observations are recorded in the logbook. This enables SCCA to maintain a complete history of every one of its drivers, and it also tells future officials what the driver's previous experience has been, what cars he has driven, and how well he has done.

At this writing SCCA safety officials have been engaged in serious discussions about even more stringent requirements for drivers who wish to go on to professional series like the Can-Am, Formula 5000 and Trans-Am. It has been possible to go through the entire SCCA licensing procedure in a Sprite and then—with an FIA license in hand—jump to Formula 5000, or Can-Am, which must be regarded as a quantum leap. There soon may be additional requirements for experience by drivers switching from the national level to international, based on horsepower ratings or some evaluation of the type of equipment they have raced.

For information about SCCA racing, write to:

Competition Director
Sports Car Club of America, Inc.
P. O. Box 22476
Denver, Colorado 80222

FIA stands for Federation Internationale de l'Automobile, which is the organization governing auto racing worldwide. The FIA is headquartered in Paris. An FIA license is required to compete in SCCA's professional racing series, the Can-Am, Formula 5000, and Trans-Am. The same license also serves as permission to race in other countries' international events and in internationally rated events in this country. They include the Grand Prix of the United States, a Formula 1 race, and the world manufacturers' championship endurance races such as the Daytona 24-hour and Watkins Glen 6-hour.

The FIA is set up as sort of a world congress, with each delegate representing a single country. In England, for instance, the Royal Automobile Club appoints its member to the FIA. In the United States, however, there are many different types of racing, many organizations involved, and such a large expanse of land covered, that a single club's representative could not do motor racing here justice.

So the major associations got together several years ago and formed a committee which represents United States interests in world motor racing. It is called the Automobile

Competition Committee of the United States (ACCUS). At this writing there are thirteen members, two each representing the five major organizations (SCCA, NASCAR, USAC, NHRA, and IMSA) and three members at large. As it might be predicted, there are constant squabbles among the various members, and at this writing USAC has moved to the brink of resignation. There will be no comment here on the merits of the dispute, but it was brought up to point out the fact that ACCUS membership has changed before and can again.

FIA listed events in this country are open to drivers who hold FIA licenses, regardless of which ACCUS member-club sanctions the race. There are exceptions to this rule, particularly in the case of USAC, but an FIA license is tantamount to an invitation to compete in all of the five major professional sanctioning bodies' races in the United States, if you can secure a ride.

For information about internationally listed events or other functions of ACCUS, write:

John Oliveau, Executive Director
Automobile Competition Committee of the U. S.
330 Vanderbilt Parkway
Hauppage, New York 11787

SCCA racing is open to every level of road racing competition from its "showroom stock" classes of sedans, for which the only modifications permitted are for safety reasons, through world championship Formula 1. Another club that is important to know about is the International Motor

Sports Association or IMSA, which stages only a limited number of events—all professional, paying prize money—for a limited range of racing cars. IMSA sanctions races for touring and grand touring cars (as defined by the FIA sporting code), some classes of formula cars, and a group termed "baby grands" that includes sub-compact sedans equipped with street tires. IMSA's technical, safety, and driver eligibility rules are quite close to those of SCCA, although it is such a new organization it has not developed such a formalized training program for beginning drivers. Until it does, the best bet for an aspiring IMSA driver is to join SCCA, go through the procedures up to the granting of an FIA license, and then apply to race with IMSA. SCCA drivers are almost always granted IMSA licenses under those circumstances.

For information about IMSA, write:

International Motor Sports Association
P. O. Box 805
Fairfield, Connecticut 06430

OVAL RACING

In the eyes of the world the most important racing organization in this country is the United States Automobile Club.

USAC sanctions the Indianapolis 500, the most important motor race and possibly the most important sporting event anywhere in this country. Within the organization of USAC that one race stands head and shoulders above every other activity in which the club is involved. The often-stated purpose of its midget and sprint car divisions is to develop young drivers, give them experience for an eventual opportunity to race at Indianapolis Motor Speedway. The entire USAC championship trail, including two other 500-mile races at Pocono and Ontario, is built around Indianapolis. The dirt track racing division is an offshoot of the championship division, a relic of the time when championship drivers competed once on the pavement at Indy and the rest of year on the dirt at smaller tracks from coast to coast. Of the racing activities not devoted exclusively to supporting the Indianapolis 500, only the stock car division remains, and even it is slanted to provide stock car racing for Indianapolis drivers. On at least two occasions USAC organized a road racing division which was unsuccessful and eventually discontinued. USAC sanction of the historic Pikes Peak Hillclimb has been discontinued. Efforts of Doug Caruthers to interest USAC in a Little League type of operation mentioned earlier in this chapter, supervising quarter-midget racing for youngsters, were discouraged. Even world record runs at Bonneville, traditionally an exclusive of USAC and its predecessor, the Contest Board of the American Automobile Association, are no longer exclusively a function of USAC. Starting in 1972, NHRA began also certifying world speed record attempts at Bonneville.

USAC is set up much like organized baseball, which has both formal and informal links to competition all the way from sandlot ball to the World Series. In USAC's typical open-wheel racing circuitry, the bottom rung is midget racing. Drivers who compete for local associations "graduate" after they reach the age of twenty-one and feel they are ready for the competition, joining the USAC midget trail. With some exceptions, midget drivers are expected to have prior experience before they can race with USAC. Sprint car drivers from outside clubs can also join USAC and go directly into the sprint car series, but they are often counseled to start at the bottom, which is midget car racing. However, a higher order of USAC license makes a top professional driver, such as A. J. Foyt or Al Unser, eligible to compete in a midget race any time he wishes. With as many as 80 races a year for the USAC midget division, it is an excellent training ground for acquiring general racing experience. There are those drivers who argue that midgets do not prepare them for what they want to do—become successful in Championship racing and go to Indianapolis. But technology is changing. There are a handful of rear-engine midgets around the country, and it is only a matter of time before they will be allowed to compete on the pavement portion of the midget championship series, just as rear-engine sprint cars are now permitted to do in that series.

The highest form of license is the one which permits a driver to compete in a Championship race. These are high-speed contests, with qualifying speeds as high as 210 miles an hour. USAC officials are very careful in accrediting drivers for this form of racing and insist on either prior USAC experience in other divisions or an FIA license, or both.

Even after becoming a Championship circuit regular a USAC driver is regarded as a rookie at the 500-mile races.

He must go through still another indoctrination and observation period, because officials rightfully feel that the history of Indianapolis proves that the 2½-mile speedway is dangerous for the inexperienced driver. Rookie procedures are slightly different and not nearly as stringent at Pocono and Ontario, but they are quite formal and institutionalized, as they are at Indianapolis.

First, USAC will not agree to accept a rookie's application to drive at Indianapolis until the track opens on about the first of May. When he reports to the speedway he fills out an application, listing his complete racing history. Usually, the rookie comes armed with recommendations from veteran race drivers and officials who have already observed him in action. In the case of USAC midget, sprint car, and Championship division drivers, these recommendations are routinely accepted, because they come from respected USAC officials and participants. In the case of SCCA and NASCAR drivers the same rules do not always apply, even though the applicant is a recognized racer of international standing. It should be pointed out, in defense of the USAC system, that there has seldom been an example of Indianapolis officials denying recognized international drivers or American super stars the opportunity to race. Drivers like Jimmy Clark, Jackie Stewart, Graham Hill, Mark Donohue, Pete Revson, and Bobby and Donnie Allison had no difficulty being accepted as capable drivers. The point is, however, that every driver who applies for permission to race at the speedway is assumed to be a knowledgeable veteran in whatever form of racing he has experienced—but he's considered a raw rookie at Indianapolis, because there is no other track like it in the world.

The first step for the rookie is a lecture, followed by a slow tour of the track in a pace car with a veteran driver who explains the idiosyncracies of the race course. He points out the racing lines, the rough spots, the slippery places, the recommended areas for safe passing, the braking points, where the caution lights and the emergency equipment are located on practice, qualifying, and race days.

The rookie is next allowed to take slow familiarization laps around the track, to see it from the driver's seat. If he is lucky, he will already have seen it during the private tests of one of the tire companies, but this is quite rare. Most rookies get their first feel of the track during the month of May.

Next, he is placed under a speed limit and allowed to work himself up to speeds prescribed during the rookie test at a rate of acceleration with which the driver feels comfortable. Officials at this point are anxious for rookies to make all deliberate haste to get up to speeds, because the track is being used at the same time by veteran drivers who are working themselves back into the groove and improving their cars. For the first few days on the track, until most of the dust is blown off, there is one overall speed limit for everybody. That's when most of the rookie practice is expected to be completed.

The rookie test—USAC doesn't call it a test, but prefers the term "rookie familiarization run"—consists of a series of ten-lap runs at specified speeds. Almost every year, as speeds have leapfrogged at the speedway, rookie standards have increased. Most recently, the first ten laps were run at 145-mile-an-hour average speeds and advanced upward in 5-mph increments to any speed over 160 mph that feels comfortable. While he is taking the test, the rookie is observed by other drivers, as well as officials, posted around the track. He is rated for his smoothness and the consistency of his lap speeds. After the test the driver is debriefed at a closed meeting, as each of the observers comments on his performance, makes suggestions and criticisms when they are appropriate.

It is difficult to write about policies of the racing officials at Indianapolis, because they are as constantly changing as the plateaus of speed. It is likewise difficult to describe the subtle interworkings of two sets of race officials, one management team appointed by the speedway and charged with the overall conduct of the race, and the other, by USAC to fill the many other necessary officiating assignments. Particularly since the safety furor in May, 1973, it is possible that conditions of change are in the offing. As for beginners on the speedway, however, if a rookie crashes or spins out before he passes his familiarization test, or if he makes some other sort of blunder that causes official concern for his safety on the race track or the safety of others, he is asked to leave the speedway, get more experience, and try again the next year. There is a lot of democracy at the policy level of the U. S. Auto Club, which is set up so that all the divergent interests of the sport are represented on its policy-making board of directors, but there is no appeal to the rulings of officials where rookies are concerned at the speedway. Safety is such a delicate possession that officials frequently act in what may seem to typical rookie drivers to be unfair ways, when officials consider safety first, aspirations of the drivers second.

It's likewise difficult to fathom the Indy mystique, without some acceptance of the fact that internal politics and strife, bitter competition among the manufacturers, the oppression of tradition, the awesome size of the crowds on qualifying and race days, personal animosities, and intense competitive spirit underlie everything. There is also the awful contemplation of big money—the high cost of racing and the rewards of victory. Indianapolis is one gigantic crapshoot, not a place for the timid or the fainthearted. If you're a young driver interested in going there, don't go to race the first time. Go to watch. Learn to understand the pressures and the meaning of financial sacrifice. There is more to racing at Indianapolis than stuffing your foot into it and turning left.

Much of the complexity, the Balkanic intrigue of Indianapolis, is a way of life with the U. S. Auto Club. USAC was formed in 1956 when the American Automobile Association decided to discontinue its sanction of motor racing events in the interest of downplaying speed and horsepower, hoping somehow that act would contribute to more safety on the highways. History proves that move was ineffective. All it accomplished was to plunge auto racing in a period of extreme turmoil. Thoughtfully concerned leaders of the sport, urged on by Tony Hulman, track president at Indianapolis, formed USAC to take over the enormous responsibilities of the AAA Contest Board. At the time AAA was sanctioning midget, sprint car, and Championship circuits, both regionally and nationally, and AAA certified all the world record runs at Bonneville. Just to corral the mustangs that had been let out of the barn, so to speak, was a huge task. While USAC was taking over the reins of leadership, other racing organizations were forming and growing rapidly. There was never a formal decision to exclude the other forms of racing these other clubs controlled, but USAC's organizers were apparently not interested in such things as road racing, stock car racing, or drag racing at the time, and when USAC did finally become interested, it was too late.

So, today, the easy way to get along in USAC is to do things USAC's way, not to "rock the boat." If you have serious aspirations to race with the nation's most prestigious club, get some experience with a local midget or sprint car organization; find out if you have talent. Then join USAC and race. The drivers who do this say it is a fantastic experience. In all the world there is no more competitive racing circuit than the USAC sprint car trail. For the sheer pleasure of wheel-to-wheel racing, nothing beats USAC midgets. Long after they should have known better, Parnelli Jones and A. J. Foyt dueled almost suicidally in midget race cars. Gary Bettenhausen risked losing one of the best rides in USAC Championship history when he defied car owner Roger Penske and raced USAC sprints and midgets (he broke an arm in a USAC sprint car race, and there was hell to pay).

For information about USAC's various racing divisions, write:

United States Auto Club
4910 West 16th Street
Indianapolis, Indiana 46224

There is another road to follow, if your ambition is to reach Indianapolis with a high level of competence in a short time and with a sense of survival appreciation that you can't find on the quarter-mile tracks of Illinois, Indiana, and Iowa, where most of the midget racing is done. That is with SCCA in an open-wheel formula car.

Formula racing is racing in a car that has no other purpose than to be raced. If you build a car to a certain international formula, it can be raced anywhere in the world. Formula cars are open-wheeled, single-seated and—almost universally—rear-engined. If you have driven a Ford and a Volkswagen, you know that cars with motors behind the driver handle differently from cars with motors in front. The same is true, but even more pronounced, in racing cars. So the progression through rear-engine formula cars is a good route to follow when driving toward Indianapolis.

Formula Vee, the slowest, cheapest, most stock and, in some estimations, most competitive formula, is the starting point for many drivers. Vee cars are powered by absolutely stock 1200cc Volkswagen engines and running gear. Components are strictly regulated so that one driver theoretically cannot get an unfair advantage through opening up his wallet and spending lavishly. At some tracks, typical Formula Vee road races start with more than fifty cars. They are a sight to behold, and the drivers say there is nothing more exhilarating than to go through tight corners three and four abreast in these relatively slow-moving racers.

For the driver who isn't satisfied with the relative snail's pace of the Vee, there is the Formula Super Vee, which is based on the 1500cc VW motor. These cars are sleeker, faster, and just as competitive because of restrictive rules. They are also more expensive to own and maintain.

Among beginners in formula road racing, the most popular car is the Formula Ford, which is based on the European 1600cc Ford motor. The Formula Ford racing car comes closest of all the under-powered machines to being a miniature Formula 1. Its speeds are much faster than those of Super Vees, and it is possible for ingenious mechanical work to provide a bit of a margin over the rest of the field, but they are still extremely competitive with each other.

Above Formula Ford on the ladder are two artificially contrived classes, Formulas B and C, which SCCA is gradually retiring in favor of the internationally recognized Formulas 2 and 3. These likewise are based on European engine formulas, but the car building restrictions are much less severe. In Europe, where Formula 2 and 3 cars are raced weekly, the competition is staggering, but in North America they are not yet popular classes.

What used to be called Formula A, an American formula because it makes use of American engines and because the cars closely resembled the pre-turbocharged Indianapolis racing machines, was adopted eagerly in Europe and came to be called Formula 5000. The term Formula 5000 comes from the fact that the engine formula calls for

5 liters of piston displacement or 5000cc. Formula 5000 cars come close to Formula 1 cars in overall performance, and, in fact, they have won combined races on occasion. A move into Formula 5000 racing on an SCCA national level, followed by graduation to the professional series, is a logical one for any Indianapolis 500 aspirant.

The final move, the traditional step for any American driver before going to Indy, is into USAC's Championship series. The Championship Trail antedates Indianapolis itself and has been the route to the American racing championship since shortly after 1900. Its list of champions is more hallowed with the names of national racing heroes than is the roll of Indianapolis winners itself—stars like Rex Mays, Earl Cooper, Harry Hartz, Ted Horn, and Tony Bettenhausen.

To break into USAC Championship racing is exceedingly tough, because car owners have so much invested in their cars they hesitate to take a chance on an unproven rookie. To have a ride that is capable of moving the young driver to the front of the pack is almost unheard of. The difference in equipment is profound, and the jump in performance from any other type of racing car is hard to describe. Turbocharged Offies, winged, aerodynamically designed skins. Incredibly wide tires. Chassis workmanship approaching art. Only the most dedicated of racing drivers can remain on the trail, including those who survive the inevitable crashes at speeds up to 200 miles an hour.

Up to this point we have discussed the mechanics of "getting into racing." There is another side of breaking into the sport, a previously unwritten code observed by all drivers and most mechanics and car owners. It covers the off-track activities of everybody in racing.

To succeed, to win, it is necessary to have the very best equipment. Equipment costs money, and money—unless you are so wealthy that racing is only an expensive hobby—must come from outside sources. That means sponsorship is required to win in nearly every case.

It is a good idea for any beginning driver to appreciate the benefits of sponsorship and to master the techniques of seeking it, holding it, and rewarding it.

A few sponsors in racing are merely paying their dues to a club which gives them enjoyment in return. They are indulging in a unique form of recreation. Some are in racing for the same reason but expect a return in terms of exposure. This class of sponsor is a little more serious about his investment, but he usually hasn't figured how his sponsorship is going to benefit him with increased business or enhanced company image or the other goals he might have in mind. He needs help, but doesn't know exactly what kind.

The good sponsor, the big-money operator who really makes it possible, with unselfish support, for an efficient racing team to produce a winner, is the one who is in racing strictly for what it can do for his business.

Unfortunately, many in racing do not understand this simple fact. As a result, many good companies are no longer available as sponsors. They have been discouraged by racing organizations that have plundered them for their money and given nothing in return. The stories of their sad experiences get around, and the reciting of them makes it difficult for others to land sponsorships.

What the driver can and must do to make sponsorship valuable to his team, and therefore to his own career, is to make his sponsorship more important to the company putting up the money. This means the driver must learn many skills unrelated to how a car is driven on a race track. We will examine some of them:

Salesmanship. To seek and find a sponsor requires the same techniques shared by the Fuller Brush man going door to door, and the corporation marketing executive closing a million-dollar deal. You must learn to sell yourself, your sport, your team in terms of what an association with it can mean for the sponor. Some drivers we have watched improve their status in racing have even taken the Dale Carnegie course or joined the Toastmasters Club (to practice public speaking), so great is their sincerity about salesmanship and improving their appearance in public. You must learn to sell yourself to the fans and to the news media, to be open and cordial, accommodating. This means you must be willing to sign autographs cheerfully, give newspaper interviews, answer innocent questions posed by the fans, and be grateful for the attention they lavish on you. You must learn to think creatively about what you can do for a sponsor and be open to his suggestions about how you can help him. You must eventually be able to speak to large groups and to engage in public relations work for race track promoters. The better PR job you do, the more will be your opportunities to earn better rides.

Unselfishness. Under the trying tension as a race approaches, every member of a racing team is coping with pressure in his own way. Human nature being what it is, petty jealousies and bickering are sometimes unavoidable. Mechanics resent the driver, who resents the team manager, who is exasperated with his mechanics. Uncontrolled, this emotional wave can engulf an entire racing team and drown it. As a driver, you must learn to recognize the signs and help prevent dissension. Sometimes the driver helps the team most by staying out of the way. Always, he helps by being available and doing what he is asked, whether it appears demeaning to him or not. It's not out of the question that a driver can pull a team together. At Bonneville, when things were going poorly, Gary Gabelich called a private meeting of the crew and announced he was going to hear everybody's gripes and try to work them all out so that the crew could start working together again. Gary scheduled a nightly meeting to consider complaints and give an audience to ideas crewmen had to improve operations. Morale picked up immediately. Suddenly, little mechanical problems stopped occurring, and less than three weeks later the "Blue Flame" had set a Land Speed Record. A racing team is a team, after all, and one element of it cannot win without the help of another.

Appreciation. After every qualifying run at Indianapolis, the driver is interviewed over the public address system. Inevitably, he recites the list of mechanics, car owners, advisers, sponsors, and friends "who made this all possible." The litany is repeated over and over, until the fans in the grandstands must have some reservations about the driver's sincerity. There is a reason for this recital. The driver really does want his mechanics to know how much he appreciates their work, and he wants them to share his brief moment of glory. But that's not the only place and the only way he can show his appreciation. One driver hanging around his racing shop might go out and buy a six-pack of beer or soda or do other little things without being asked, while another may say, "See ya tomorrow," and head for the golf course. The effects on team morale are often obvious. Being aware of the feelings of others can go a long way toward making you a successful racing driver.

"Cool." Inevitably, there will be some injustice inflicted upon the race driver. A car owner drops you because another driver "bought his way" onto the team. An official ruling goes against you when the true facts do not justify it. The tire company seems to be giving other drivers better tires than you are able to get. Your first instinct is to blow off steam. More often than not, that is the wrong move. Letting your fists do the talking in a beef with another driver, official, or mechanic is even worse. Stories about the hot-headed actions of certain drivers follow them all during their careers. Officials and news reporters can't help resurrecting stories like those every time a driver gets himself in some new difficulty. Maintaining an outward calm in the face of unjustified wrongs usually pays dividends. This is not to mean you should lie down and let someone else run over you. Fight back, if that's the right move at that moment, but don't, under any circumstances, lose your temper. That moment when you indulge your temper will come back eventually to haunt you.

Personal habits. Your private life is your own and should be kept that way. It's not the purpose of this book to lecture on morals, only to caution that some excesses can be detrimental to your ability behind the wheel; and some activities which are considered immoral can be harmful to your career in racing if they are made public or if you purposely flaunt them. The great motocross champion, Rolf Tibblin, once observed an experiment in Sweden in which a rider deliberately became intoxicated after timing his laps the day before. The next day, sober again but suffering from the inevitable hangover, he attacked the same course on his bike, only to lap much slower and make many more mistakes. The lesson was clear to Tibblin; and although there is no scientific evidence to back it up as far as auto racing is concerned, the suspicion is that you cannot perform as well the morning after a prolonged bout of drinking. Likewise, there is no place in racing for the fool who takes dope or pills. He is racing toward trouble. As far as some of the other problems a driver faces, the most serious is posed by the camp follower. Veteran drivers know their opportunities for sexual conquest are unlimited. Most have the good sense to keep their relationships private and out of the public eye. Some, to their later regret, do not. Parading the latest lover before the fans and the other racers may be ego-satisfying, but it's actually degrading. More important, the addition of a non-racing responsibility to the confusion of race day is distracting and could have an adverse effect on your performance. Drivers who really have their heads screwed on right kiss their sweethearts goodbye in the morning and don't think about them until after the track closes for the day.

Dedication. Nobody succeeds in any sport unless he works at it. A true champion defends his title twenty-four hours a day. Driving requires physical ability, sharp reflexes, mental alertness, mechanical knowledge, and emotional discipline. Winning requires dedication. If a 100 percent commitment to auto racing seems a bit chauvinistic to you, you are a hobbyist. Just go out and enjoy yourself, but don't try to make a career out of racing, because you will fail. To be a winner requires enormous personal sacrifice, and there are few human beings who have both the ability and desire to reach the top. You may not be one of the few. But then again, you may.

8

Looking into the Crystal Ball

Contemplating the future is a fascinating pastime. Literature is loaded with speculation about it—More's *Utopia,* Verne's *20,000 Leagues Under the Sea,* Wells' *1984.* Politicians, television commentators, and college professors dote on predictions. Ministers speak weekly about the hereafter. Sports pages are loaded with predictions, odds, point spreads, pre-game statements, analyses, charts, and picking contests. Many people still shell out their money for the speculation of fortune tellers, and many more indulge in astrological forecast.

To predict what will happen to the high-performance driving cars on street and track, it is necessary to have a special clairvoyance, because so many new developments are affecting the transportation industry and the automobile itself on a day-to-day basis. Some observers see a dismal future for the automobile, which is under attack for its adverse effects on the environment, the horrendous safety statistics, the energy crisis, the eventual exhaustion of this planet's metallurgical and petroleum resources, and the sanity of the entire industrial revolution. Will the automobile be outlawed at some future date? Will America's greatest freedom, freedom of choice, be eroded in the name of environmental protection? Will inflation of costs and taxes eventually make it impossible for the average person to own a motor car? Will auto racing be outlawed, for safety or ecological reasons?

To delve into these and other questions will give only clues to an uncertain future. In order to examine the whole question of high performance driving, it is necessary to look at our most recent past experience and try to speculate on where the trends of public policy and private practice are leading us.

GOVERNMENT

For a nation of people so passionately in love with the idea of individual liberty, the United States has moved with shocking speed toward the suppression of individual desires and toward a planned and ordered society, with government dictating a lot in terms of lifestyle.

The Environmental Protection Agency, for example, almost threatens the prohibition of automobile traffic in major metropolitan areas. The Council of Economic Advisers tampers with the laws of supply and demand in such a way that prices of gasoline, new and used cars, and repair parts fluctuate erratically. To put it another way, the traditional laws of supply and demand do not operate freely.

Congress and various state legislatures flirt with the idea of lowering speed limits to force motorists to conserve fuel. Anticipating a smog alert, federal offices shut down for the day with the aim of reducing air pollution by cutting traffic flow during the commuter rush hours on the freeways. California, soon to be followed by other states, demands installation of pollution control devices on used cars. The NHTSA, prodded by the Ralph Nader-inspired consumerists, goads auto manufacturers into developing the so-called "passive restraint," the air bag—a safety device that is supposed to work whether you want it to or not.

At the state level, it seems inevitable that those environmental and consumerist issues not touched upon by the federal government will become fair game for a variety of new regulations. As reported by the Specialty Equipment Manufacturers Association, several states have already gone in for noise legislation affecting the motor vehicle and some are experimenting with laws which make it illegal to add speed or safety modifications to a car which alter or replace components put there by the factory. These laws virtually make it illegal for an automobile to be upgraded to a better condition, even to a condition in which it pollutes less than it did in stock condition or is safer or is quieter.

Noise legislation is customarily vague, subject to the whims of police charged with enforcing it. SEMA and other concerned industry groups are opposing laws of this type wherever they emerge. Air pollution control, however, is a more serious matter, and the outlaw of speed equipment is a threat to the part of the automotive aftermarket which supplies enthusiasts. While SEMA is actively opposing laws introduced in individual states every time they come to public notice, keeping track of the problem is like trying to keep water from leaking out of a sieve. In the future, it may be possible for a motorist to be stopped by a traffic officer who would issue a citation because his exhaust system wasn't installed by the factory. That's true repression, and the only important representative of the motorist fighting it today is SEMA.

To lessen the threat to individual liberty, SEMA has adopted two strategies. One is to co-operate with authorities in the drafting of reasonable laws, laws that allow optional performance and safety accessories on motor cars so long as they are equal or superior to original equipment in terms of air pollution or safety. The other is to lobby against bad legislation, and there is a lot of it. When laws are passed that interfere with the rights of enthusiasts, in the opinion of SEMA, the organization encourages court tests of those laws and assists by providing as much information to enthusiasts in litigation as it can, short of providing legal defense.

If you, in your state, believe that pending legislation or a law already on the books unnecessarily penalizes you because you are an automotive enthusiast, contact SEMA for guidance and possible assistance with the problem. Write:

Specialty Equipment Manufacturers Association
11001 East Valley Mall, Suite 204
El Monte, California 91731

Industry reacts to government fiat as surely as private citizens do and often is more effective in working change. There is as much grumbling in corporate board rooms as there is at the corner beer parlor, beauty shop, or the high-school cafeteria. What Americans have to decide in the decades immediately ahead is how much government control is good for the country, how far it can go without impairing our desirable liberties, and with what wisdom the government can be counted on to employ those controls. The large corporations make no secret of their disdain for government interference with their affairs, and it remains to be seen if the general public will become as concerned. Only at that point will the trend toward a more regulative government change.

Public attitudes are difficult to gauge, even by opinion polls, because they are constantly shifting. In California, for instance, 1972 was a year when motorists were united in their clamor for something to be done about automobile-created smog. Their legislators gave them a retrofit smog device program, but when it came time to put it into effect there was a groundswell of public sentiment against starting the program. While pollution control officials were studying possible adverse effects of smog devices on car engines, the worst of the smog season in the state was in progress and there was a shift in attitude again. Legislators, newspaper and television editorial writers, and environmental groups urged the state to get on with its project to clean up the older cars. The NHTSA has been telling Americans for several years that drunks on the highways are involved in half the fatal accidents. Should the safety establishment ever seriously attempt to remove these drunks from the driving population, there could be a serious public reaction against that move.

Cure-alls, in other words, are not in the cards. Hopefully,

a lot of the changes in the automobile, driving, traffic safety, smog control, and motor recreation will be made by the private sector and not by government. Only time will tell.

EDUCATION

Experts say that the main barrier to improvement of driver training is money. It is a formidable one. It implies that public money is needed, which in turn means more taxes. The reality of public spending is that better teaching of new drivers is well down on the list of government priorities. The squalor of the big cities is a far bigger public problem in terms of millions of people living their lives in hopeless poverty, while 50,000 or so are killed on the highways. So it is unlikely that the NHTSA, or any other federal agency, is going to do anything soon to make the various states upgrade their driver training programs.

Surely, there would be criticism from the media of upgrading driver training, as there was recently when *Time* Magazine pointed scornfully to a college which listed on its faculty a professor of driver training. Only a handful of enthusiast magazines, such as *Car & Driver, Car Craft, Cars,* and *Road & Track,* have bothered to treat the subject with more than an off-hand mention, and if you can't get the buff books interested in a subject like this, how are you going to enlist the aid of CBS or the *New York Times* in helping to shape public opinion on the matter? There is widespread apathy toward both the problem of highway safety and this aspect of the solution.

Finally, the safety establishment would feel threatened if it were subjected to the hypothesis that one of the main reasons for accidents on public roads is that it had not adequately prepared drivers for using them in the first place. Two generations of traffic cops have been brainwashed with "speed kills!" nonsense, and it is unlikely they could be brought to see the real causes of driver failure resulting in the awful carnage permitted today.

While it is not likely that driver education will improve noticeably in the next few years, there are some indications that experiments and research will show the need. Plans are on the drawing boards in Washington to study accident records of well-coached drivers against those of the average thirty-and-six high-school student, to see what their experience on the road has been over a number of years. Results will be long range, if significant at all, but they may point to the obvious conclusion that something must be done to improve driver proficiency beyond the use of accelerator, brake, and turn signal taught in driver ed classes.

One suggestion is that on the junior college level some high-performance driver training coures will be offered to teach prospective instructors, who some years down the line will, in turn, be capable of operating skid schools and teaching high-speed control, proper cornering, survival driving, and evasive maneuvering. The problem once more is money, because this type of special training requires large paved areas away from public highways, such as Bondurant uses at his school in California. The need for facilities implies the need for paved expanses of land, which in metropolitan areas are very costly. On the other hand, to train future instructors would be meaningless if the government were not planning to use their special skills to train future students. Such training would require even more facilities, special vehicles, and more time devoted to learning by beginning drivers. Ken Dunipace of the NHTSA claims the cost is staggering to contemplate, possibly so high that taxpayers might not stand for it.

THE AUTOMOBILE

If Ralph Nader and some environmentalists get their way, there won't be any automobiles in thirty years. If costs of operation, insurance, and original purchase price continue to escalate, only the rich will be able to afford them in that time. None of these possibilities seem logical, because the freedom to transport oneself wherever the mood strikes is too deeply a part of the American way of life. It would seem that we will have automobiles in some form or another for many years—until some better form of personal transportation comes along.

It also seems that the automobile will not change very much except to adapt to the conditions imposed by such realities as the energy crisis, pollution control, the safety problem, and changing transportation needs of a changing population.

A shortage of gasoline, particularly in the near future, will create a demand for cars which are more economical to operate. Compacts and subcompacts are capturing a larger share of the automobile sales dollar each year, because they are smaller, are simpler to maintain, use less fuel, and handle better. Oil industry observers say that the gasoline retail price will rise to more than a dollar per gallon in a few years, a level it reached many years ago in Europe. At that price, cars which deliver 30 miles per gallon will be very popular, and the rolling battleships so in vogue during the '50s and '60s will recede in public acceptance.

Today the energy crisis, or fuel shortage, and the demands of pollution control technology appear to be on collision courses. The public is asked to use less fuel, but fit-on smog devices gulp extra fuel by their very application. It would seem that improved technology will solve this problem in time, if past experience means anything. The second generation of smog devices will be better integrated into the internal combustion engine than the first, the third better than the second, and so on. Finally, automotive technology ought to supply the motorist with a clean engine that is more efficient than its dirty antecedents. Instead of paying a fuel penalty or giving poorer performance as they do now, clean engines of the future may some day produce better fuel mileage and performance. Solutions may not be far down the line. One approach was suggested by Andy Granatelli during a conversation in his motel room at Indianapolis not long ago:

"Look where we have come in forty years of automobile history," he said. "We had the Model A, which gave us twenty-five miles a gallon and more. It was clean and simple to take care of. I would bet that a Model A could pass, or come close to passing, the emission standards today.

"So what did we do? We kept making engines bigger, cars bigger, faster, dirtier, and heavier. Now we get five to eight miles a gallon and produce dirty air. It's insanity."

Without saying it in so many words, Granatelli was predicting the American automobile manufacturer may soon turn to the simplicity of the Model A to rediscover many long-shelved solutions to modern problems. A lot of new cars today are sold with four-cylinder engines, no frills, all dedicated to the business of going from one place to another with efficiency. There is a generation of exciting vehicles, though not all four-cylinder models, that have simplicity as a theme—exemplified by the Pinto, the Gremlin, the Audi, and the Jensen Healey.

A trend toward bigness in cars suggested by Nader and another safety theorist, Dr. William Haddon, may have been sidetracked by the fuel crisis. If Dr. Haddon gets his way, in a few years the only vehicles in the showrooms would be 7000- to 10,000-pound tanks like those ludicrous Experimental Safety Vehicles (ESVs) produced for the government by AMF and Fairchild. The theory behind those cars was that protection was needed for the occupants in any crash, because the assumption had to be made that despite all the safety precautions in the world they would crash. Dr. Haddon and the champion of the ESVs, Douglas Toms, neglected to account for the corrolary—any other vehicle crashing into as big a tub as the ESV would be in great jeopardy.

The trouble with making laws to regulate automobile engineering is that it ignores the reality of a hundred million cars and trucks already in service, and concentrates on the ten million to be sold new each year. The logic, unfortunately, had no effect on the fate of the ESV program; only the fuel shortage that made overweight cars obsolete before they ever reached the showroom put an end to this weird solution to the traffic safety problem.

Another factor not addressed by the planners of an increasingly meddlesome government bureaucracy is the population trend away from large families and toward zero population growth. It's something the government has had little or nothing to do with. For hundreds of years government has been trying to legislate morals without success. It appears that science, cooperating with economic forces, has changed the attitudes of large numbers of Americans about family living. Families in the near future will be smaller, creating a different demand for family transportation. How this will affect the future of the automobile is bound to be felt quite profoundly.

Smaller families lessen the demand for lots of interior seating in cars, but having fewer children to raise gives young families more time and money for recreation. The automobile industry will be greatly influenced by these conditions for at least the next twenty years.

On the basis of all these divergent influences, it is difficult to predict what cars will be like in the future; how tough it will be to own them; whether pollution control will become a sufficiently pressing demand to severely curtail automobile use; whether mass transit will become so efficient that car ownership will not be as desirable; or if oppressive government regulations will discourage car ownership. It is very likely that the next couple of generations will take a more serious approach to the automobile and that the car will become more of a no-nonsense possession than a sex symbol or a token of conspicuous consumption. More cars will be smaller, and technology, coupled with consumer demand, will make them safer and more fun to drive.

ECONOMICS

This country has not experienced the horrendous upheaval of a major depression for thirty-five years, and our leaders keep assuring everybody they have learned how to head off economic calamities of that magnitude. That may be so, but leadership has failed to deliver before on other crucial issues. If we ever go through another severe depression, heaven help the automobile industry.

Assuming that will never happen, we are apparently faced with a continuous rate of inflation, a spiral which has been only temporarily interrupted a few times in the last hundred years. Costs will climb. Taxes will climb. Eventually, automobiles could be priced out of the means of the average motorist. This could occur quite soon, if such government-dictated new-car features as the exhaust catalyst are required, and if the "safety car" crashability add-ons are forced on us.

MAINTENANCE

This country is in the midst of an almost unnoticed crisis—a critical shortage of trained mechanics. While we suffer from the lack of competent mechanical labor, vehicles are becoming more complicated with smog devices and auxiliary systems. Thanks to the bungling of Detroit's automotive engineers years ago, probably dictated by company expediency, many late model cars are so difficult to work on that a terrible amount of time is wasted unbolting one part of the engine to get to another.

Even though the manufacturers seem barely interested in this problem today, one can only hope they will begin to remove one of the important barriers to good maintenance of automobiles by improving the design of the engine compartment to make each component easier to service. Any quick examination under the hood will confirm the suspicion that most Detroit products were designed by a committee of stylists who stood around and figured out where to squeeze in this new accessory or that.

The industry and the public at large share in the blame for not making a career in auto mechanics as glamorous and desirable as it might be. Any good mechanic will tell you that he can make a comfortable living without having to strain himself or can become wealthy by working hard, but many good mechanics are overworked because of the shortage in the labor pool.

In recent years the factories have tried to recruit young mechanics. They have been assisted by the armed forces and the poverty program, which have trained mechanics at government expense. The shortage, however, becomes more acute each year.

Complicating the problem is the advent of consumerism. Rightly so, consumer advocates have pointed the finger of accusation at shady repair garage operators who practice fraud and deceit on the public. In California, sale of unneeded parts and service is said to be the number one fraud by the Consumer Affairs Administration.

Under the circumstances, it is hard for a young person choosing a career to get a lot of enthusiasm whipped up to become a mechanic when he becomes aware of the public image of the trade. In the long run, however, the auto repair industry may be the better for current efforts to clean it up and—once purged of scoundrels—may better be able to recruit good talent.

AUTO RACING

It has been said that when the first racing car leaps over the fence at Indianapolis or Daytona and crashes into the stands killing fifty or a hundred spectators, that will be the last auto race allowed to be held in this country. The sport hangs on just such a tenuous thread.

Salt Walther came very close to doing just that at Indianapolis in 1973, when fuel from his crashing race car sprayed several rows of spectators and put twelve persons in the hospital. As expected, the press and public reaction was one of shock and horror. The *New York Times* called for outlawing the sport.

The bitter reality, as far as racing enthusiasts are concerned, is that until major safety innovations are made for Indianapolis cars (they haven't been, despite the publicity), the danger of a racing car flipping into the grandstands is ever present.

Many critics of the sport, almost all of whom admit they dislike racing altogether, attack it for more than danger. Ecologists find the continuation of auto racing untenable in the face of an energy crisis. To them it's like lighting a match to the last few gallons left at the gas pump. Pseudo-safety experts believe racing encourages wild behavior on the highways, although there is conflicting evidence on this point. The noise produced by motor racing is offensive to persons who live close to tracks where it is held, and anti-noise legislation is getting more attention in many states.

Auto racing is also overpopulated with tracks, a situation which is likely to change due to economic conditions. In California alone there are more than a hundred places where motor races are regularly held. Ten years from now there are not likely to be more than sixty. As the result of consolidation and the elimination of weaker track operations, auto racing may become such big business that it will be able to survive in what is becoming an increasingly hostile atmosphere. While critics on all sides are attacking the sport, there are still those loyal 45 million or so fans who continue to support it by paying for tickets to see it. Television exposure is increasing, and the audience is broadening.

It seems safe to say that if nobody rides that airborne race car into the grandstands, auto racing will continue to prosper and may become the dominant sport of the '70s, as it was predicted at the start of this decade.

THE MASTER DRIVERS LICENSE

The term of this idea was spread by Doug Toms and his aides. The MDL was eagerly accepted by enthusiasts and grudgingly studied by the safety establishment. Perhaps the concept is far ahead of its time.

Different presidents will come and go in Washington. They will appoint different men to head the NHTSA. Different policies will come into vogue. We can only hope that each time a change is made, the MDL proposal will be taken out of a filing cabinet somewhere in the Department of Transportation Building and reviewed. It has great merit.

The Master Drivers License calls for a stiffer licensing procedure to create a recognized new level of driving proficiency. The details have never been worked out, but the concept is to require attendance at a high-performance school similar to Bondurant's and then base the licensing test on extreme driving conditions and special skills needed to cope with them.

Just what the government envisions as the reward for holding a Master Drivers License is not yet clear. Toms foresaw special insurance discounts, permission to drive certain special vehicles, and a sort of status that would make holding an MDL desirable. To be effective, it will take more than that.

California, for example, has already experimented with dedicating certain lanes of the freeway exclusively to buses. If that were followed in the case of MDL holders, some unlimited speed lanes on the interstate system might be restricted to superior vehicle operators.

There are a few incorrigible drivers who seem to lack the ability to stay out of trouble on the street. Traffic court judges could require them to take periodic courses that lead to the MDL as a condition of probation. That would seem to be more effective than showing them horror movies depicting gory crashes, which is the practice today.

MDL holders might have a degree of immunity from harassment by traffic police, if such a privilege is practical. Completion of an MDL course might entitle the younger driver to full driving privileges sooner or to waiver of insurance premium cost penalties imposed on him.

The idea that insurance companies will volunteer discounts to better high-performance drivers is ridiculous, in view of the insurance industry's head-in-the-sand attitude toward traffic safety over the years. Statistics developed by the NHTSA prove that insurance companies have been wrong in their contention that a small number of drivers causes a large number of accidents. Yet, rates continue to be based on this fallacy. Insurance companies also perpetuate the myth that drivers who collect traffic citations are accident prone. Their rate schedules reflect this belief. The worst inference of all made by insurance companies is that certain attitudes of drivers can be detected by discovering what sort of car a motorist owns. The oppressive rate schedule assessed against owners of so-called "muscle cars" destroyed the market for a type of car that was inherently safer and usually better maintained than any other group in the general car population. Statistics which were used to show that hot car owners are involved in more accidents actually only proved that they were younger and more inexperienced. The Master Drivers License concept would theoretically control the problem by requiring owners of this sort of car to hold an MDL before they could purchase one.

One of the first benefits of a Master Drivers License program would be to require all police and other emergency vehicle drivers to pass the requirements in order to keep their jobs. Only a few states have any sort of special training for emergency vehicle drivers. California, which is one of the leaders in this field, held an emergency conference on the subject in 1972, a meeting at which officials expressed shock and dismay over the fact that the state's standards for such training were almost non-existent. Aside from the Bondurant school, the California Highway Patrol training course, a police pursuit training school at Pomona, and a new course for police at Orange County International Raceway, there are almost no courses available for emergency vehicle drivers in the state. And California sets the pace for the rest of the country.

Just what form the MDL will eventually take is anybody's guess. It's a great plan and needs wider discussion to shape its future. To become effective, it will have to be adopted by all 50 states, not just by the federal government. That will take years, and the process will not begin until somebody dusts off the file and puts it on the top of his desk in Washington. It will be interesting to see if a good idea like this ever sees the light of day.

TRAFFIC ENFORCEMENT

Along with the trend toward more repressive control of our freedom-loving population, the safety law enforcers are getting very sophisticated and thorough in their methods. Modern technology has contributed devices that will clock passing cars no matter what direction they are going. Radar devices, once outlawed by judges who considered their use as illegal entrapment, are widely accepted. Creeping Big Brotherism is all the rage in the towns and hamlets from coast to coast. Traffic citations are big business.

A California state legislator was caught one night in a radar trap in Sacramento at 10 miles an hour over the speed limit. Sacramento's city government rues the day that man was ticketed. As most of us would be, the lawmaker was incensed at being stopped for so little reason. The streets were almost deserted. He wasn't creating a safety hazard. He was driving at the same speed he had observed other cars drive on the same street at other times. He hadn't been drinking. He was alone in his car, and to his way of thinking, he was acting like a responsible citizen.

The next day at his office he began the process of information gathering that led to a law he introduced, a law which eventually may have a profound effect on all traffic enforcement from coast to coast.

The facts he gathered were these: Sacramento was collecting nearly a million dollars a year in traffic fines, one of its largest single sources of municipal revenue. Over a period of years the accident rate and the traffic fatality rate had increased in the city, despite these so-called efforts at improving safety. He concluded that the entrapment of motorists served no useful purpose in the control of accidents.

As a result of his research, he introduced a bill to prevent cities from using unreasonable entrapment methods specifically designed to make money from traffic fines. That was the beginning of a new approach to traffic enforcement in the state. The California Highway Patrol soon adopted a new policy of ignoring minor traffic violations, ordering its officers to make themselves more visible, and cracking down on obviously unsafe drivers. The CHP soon found that it was getting more productive use of its officers, who were not constantly tied up writing meaningless speeding tickets, Perhaps coincidentally, perhaps as a result, traffic accident statistics improved in the first few months the new policy was followed.

Such enlightened, imaginative traffic safety management is not likely to sweep the country like wildfire. However, if some of the CHP's assumptions are borne out by experience, the rest of the country may take notice. Eventually, we may all benefit from the application of sane traffic enforcement methods.

THE DRUNK DRIVING MENACE

We have already discussed in an earlier chapter the reasons why judges don't simply sweep all the booze fighters off the streets. They can't, unless they put them all in jail and keep them there. Alcoholism is a disease, one which has increasingly serious social consequences. The NHTSA's initial approach was to treat the disease for what it is, to rehabilitate the alcoholic and let his sobriety correct his poor driving performance. While it is too soon to tell if its program of establishing Alcohol Safety Action Programs (ASAP) is going to be effective, the project has been enthusiastically accepted by all segments of the safety establishment as well as sociologists and the medical profession.

Treating individual drunk drivers for their emotional and medical problems is a long and complicated procedure. It is doubtful that any benefits will be noticeable for many years. In the meantime, our advice stands—don't drive while drunk, and stay out of the way of those who do.

HIGH-PERFORMANCE DRIVING SCHOOLS

In the absence of public policy that requires high-performance driver training, the Bob Bondurants of this world should prosper. Unfortunately, this type of school is based on personalized instruction, the most expensive kind, and that means the cost must remain high to individual students. Consequently, only a limited few with the money to spend will ever be able to afford the great experience of learning to drive a racing car and learning to react to catastrophic driving situations.

If you love driving, if you want to go into racing, if you can somehow scrape together the money, the experience is worth the expense. One week with Bondurant is worth a year of experience on the street. It's worth more, because that year is not likely to subject you to crash conditions and skids, except under very unusual circumstances.

If you're a parent and have a child with aptitude for high-performance driving, encourage him or her by sending your child to a special school. As any veteran traffic policeman will tell you, the kid is going to drive fast anyway. You might as well equip him with the knowledge necessary to survive.

The hypocritical truth about traffic safety is that everybody gives lip service to speed limits and slogans, but very few motorists apply standards to their own driving which they want everybody else to observe. As long as this is so, learning how to drive at the limits of your own ability is a practical course to follow. It could save your life.

Index

Index

Index